CLIFFE KNECHTLE

GIVE ME AN ANSWER

THAT SATISFIES MY HEART & MY MIND

Answers to
Your Toughest
Questions about
Christianity

Foreword by Leighton Ford

INTERVARSITY PRESS
DOWNERS GROVE, ILLINOIS 60515

InterVarsity Press is the book-publishing division of Inter-Varsity Christian Fellowship, a student movement active on campus at hundreds of universities, colleges and schools of nursing. For information about local and regional activities, write IVCF, 233 Langdon St., Madison, WI 53703.

Cover photograph: Steve Falk
Illustrations: Dave Zentner

ISBN 0-87784-569-7

Printed in the United States of America

Library of Congress Cataloging in Publication Data

Knechtle, Cliffe, 1954—
  Give me an answer that satisfies my heart and my mind.

  Includes bibliographies.
    1. Apologetics—20th century—Miscellanea.
  2. Theology—Miscellanea.   I. Title.
  BT1105.K6   1986   230   86-10549
  ISBN 0-87784-569-7

---

17 16 15 14 13 12 11 10 9 8
99 98 97 96 95 94 93 92 91

In the beginning God created the family. Jesus taught us to pray, "Our Father . . ." My earthly father and mother, Emilio and Ann, introduced my five younger brothers and sisters and me to our Heavenly Father. The Lord has shown me different facets of his love and truth through David, Grace, Heidi, John, Stuart and his wife Mary Banks. Through marriage I have been adopted into the loving family of Stuart and Dorothy McDonald, Kirk and Donna, Jim and Susan, Trey and Mary, Clay, and Bonnie. My wife, Sharon, has been my strongest supporter and encourager. Her love and joy, frequently in the face of bitter rejection, have been a window through which many have seen Jesus.
This book is dedicated to my family.

Acknowledgments

I wish to thank a group of individuals who have been used by God to influence this book and Sharon's and my life.

Pete Hammond, Evangelism Director for Inter-Varsity Christian Fellowship, and his wife, Shirley, have poured love, energy, godly wisdom, humor and a healthy fear of stupid mistakes into our lives.

Doug Whallon is the reason I am on Inter-Varsity staff. His counsel and friendship over the years have been invaluable. His wife, Mary, and he have taught Sharon and me much about marriage.

Keith and Molly Dunn travel in a truck around the country preparing campuses for the open-air meetings. Their servant attitudes, zealousness for the Lord and friendship make them one of God's greatest gifts to Sharon and me.

Andy Le Peau and Bill Chickering have spent hours refining the manuscript of this rookie author.

Inter-Varsity staff are committed to teaching students how to live under the lordship of Jesus Christ and how to study the Word of God. It is the highest privilege to work with such a group of people in building the kingdom of Christ. Mike and Gina Basler, John and Alice Bower, Ann Beyerlein, Hunter and Julie Dockery, Don and Joanne Fields, Hollis and Susan Kim, Rob and Sherry Knight, Joel and Linda Olson, Paul and Cheryl Sharps, Paul and Karen Sorrentino, Mack and Leeanne Stiles, Larry and Nina Thiel, Paul and Margaret Tokunaga, Pete Wilson, and Jeanette Yep have been good listeners and able counselors as we have fought together against the idols of our culture and have proclaimed the risen Christ.

Gordon MacDonald, president of Inter-Varsity Christian Fellowship, has been a consistent encourager in spite of an intensely hectic schedule.

Dr. and Mrs. William Wood have been most generous to Sharon and me. Dr. Wood's help in thinking through difficult questions has been invaluable.

Without the prayers and financial partnership of our supporters, proclaiming Christ in the open air on college campuses would have been a short-lived exercise. I want to thank them for their faithfulness.

Foreword

The Apostle Peter told the early Christians to be "prepared to give an answer to everyone who asks you to give the reason for the hope that you have" (1 Pet 3:15). Cliffe Knechtle helps us to do just that.

Out of the firsthand experience of hundreds of encounters on campuses and other settings, Cliffe has picked the questions he most hears and the answers that have meant most to him and his hearers. I believe his book will be a great help both to seekers who want to know more about Christ and to Christians who want to know better how to communicate Christ.

Jesus Christ calls us to follow him in faith—but not in blind faith. He asks not for belief without evidence, but for commitment without reservation. So he tells us to love God with all our mind as well as with all our heart and strength.

Answers in themselves may not convert anyone, but they can help to clear up honest doubts (or to remove less than honest excuses) so we can face the total claims of Jesus on our lives and wills.

Cliffe doesn't pose as an intellectual. But then most of us are not intellectuals. Yet we do have seeking hearts and inquiring minds. Behind this book is a young man who himself has been gripped by Jesus. That makes *Give Me an Answer* compelling. When I read it, I can still see in my mind Cliffe as a college student playing basketball in our back yard. (And he was much better than he gives himself credit for. I hardly ever saw him miss a jump shot!) He writes and he speaks with the same intensity and commitment with which he played ball.

But it is an intense love for Jesus Christ that shines forth here. Evangelism—communicating the life of Christ—is not Cliffe's job. It is his passion, a passion to make Christ mean everything to each of us who reads.

Leighton Ford
Charlotte, North Carolina
June 1986

Introduction

My friends in high school had anything they wanted. If one of the guys I played sports with wanted sex, they found a girl to go to bed with. If they wanted a new car, they bought it. If they wanted to go swimming, they simply stepped out to the pool in their back yard. One friend was the son of an executive vice president of an insurance corporation in Manhattan. But despite all of his wealth, he jumped off the Golden Gate Bridge in San Francisco screaming, "I'm free, I'm free."

Another high-school friend was the son of an executive vice president of a New York bank. All his possessions and experiences did him little good when his body was wheeled into the morgue. He died of a drug overdose.

Maybe you can see why I grew to hate sin so much. I'm not against having a good time. But I care for my friends and my family. And I will do whatever I can to keep such unnecessary pain out of their lives. My friends had it all—all except a deep relationship with the living God. They did not fill the God-shaped vacuum that each of us has in our lives. Instead, they gorged themselves on the world's pleasures and ended up empty. This is why I have such a strong desire to reach out to my friends and to introduce them to the closest friend I have, the Lord Jesus Christ.

This desire stayed with me when I went to Davidson College in North Carolina. One of my goals at Davidson was to play basketball. And I did. I played on the Davidson basketball team each and every practice. And at every game I had a great seat—the bench.

I wanted to tell my teammates about Christ, but I was the worst player on the team. I never started. I wondered if it wouldn't be easier to tell them about God if I was the best player, but God taught me that in my weakness his strength would be made perfect. God didn't call me to be a superstar. He didn't call me to be famous. He called me to be a faithful ambassador for Jesus Christ. I learned that if I would be faithful, God would work through me.

During my years at Davidson I was privileged to get to know Leighton and Jean Ford. They had a son named Sandy who was deeply committed to Christ. We had many good times together. But it was to end too soon. In 1981 Sandy died on the operating table during open-heart surgery.

Shortly after his son's death, Leighton said to me, "Cliffe, at times I feel like going out into the woods, lying down and dying." Few of us will ever understand the pain Leighton and Jean have gone through in losing their son. But I watched Leighton continue to faithfully preach the gospel in spite of the intense hurt he was experiencing. He would stand in front of a group of people and tell them, "God loves you. He has proven it by sending Christ to die in your place." And all the time he was grieving deeply over the loss of his own flesh and blood. But Leighton and Jean were faithful. Everything in life didn't turn out the way they might have chosen. But they continued to reach out, and God is using them mightily today to build his kingdom.

Leighton and Jean taught me that our lives are not to be based on feelings. Our lives are to be based on commitments. We are first of all to remain strong in our commitment to Jesus Christ. Second, we are to be strong in our commitment to our family. And third, we are to be strong in our commitment to reaching a world that does not know God's love.

After graduating from Davidson, I went to Gordon-Conwell Theological Seminary. While there I prayed that God would open up the doors for me to preach the gospel. No invitations came. I became frustrated and prayed harder. One night as I was praying, the Holy Spirit convicted me, "Cliffe, if your desire is to stand in front of a group of people, wag your tongue and have them slap you on the back and tell you what a fine job you did, then you have major problems. Your real desire had better be to reach people for Christ in any way possible."

Suddenly I realized that my lack of faith was the roadblock. I figured if I wanted to reach the people who went to bars, that's where I should go too. So I decided to go there and talk about Jesus Christ and not wait for an invitation.

I'll never forget the first night I preached in an inner-city bar in Boston. I parked my car, got out and headed toward the tavern. The closer I got, the more intimidated I became. By the time I reached the bar I was so scared I kept right on walking. For two hours I walked around the block trying to gather the courage to go into the bar and tell those people about Christ. Finally I said, "Cliffe, you are defeated. Go back to the seminary."

As I opened my car door, the Holy Spirit stopped me. "Cliffe, why don't you want to go preach in that bar? There are two reasons: first of all, you're afraid they're going to think you are a religious fanatic. But Cliffe, whose image are you trying to polish? You had better be living to polish the image of the Lord Jesus Christ, not your own. Second, you're afraid that someone is going to take a shot at you. You're afraid you might be hurt. But you have placed your life in the hands of the living God and he has promised never to leave you, fail you or forsake you."

Those thoughts struck me forcefully. So I turned around, walked into the bar and said, "Excuse me, gentlemen, the apostle John writes in 1 John 4:10, 'This is love: not that we loved God, but that he loved us and sent his Son as an atoning sacrifice for our sins.' "

The bartender came at me, cursing at the top of his voice. I said, "Excuse me, sir. All I want to do is talk with these men about what means most in life—knowing God as a friend."

The bartender replied, "Do you want to know what God is? God is the cash register. All I care about these men is the money they have in their pockets." I couldn't believe he said it so bluntly.

Every weekend after that I would bring seminary friends down with me to inner-city Boston. They would go into a bar and I would come in ten minutes later. At times a hush would fall across the place as I preached. Usually I was kicked out. But after I left, my seminary friends would talk with people one-to-one about Jesus Christ.

One night I was driving home after preaching in a bar. Suddenly, I had to twist my steering wheel to avoid missing a man who was lying half on the sidewalk and half on the street. A hundred feet past that man, the Holy Spirit showed me that I was the hypocrite in Jesus' parable of the good Samaritan. Yes, I could talk to people about Jesus, but when it came to rearranging my schedule and helping a man who was lying in the gutter, I was too busy. I put the car in reverse, went back to the man, bought him a meal and brought him to a place to stay for the night.

Joy comes from serving others, from reaching out to those who are hurting. God knocked me out of my apathy and indifference toward the needs of hurting people. I found great satisfaction in working among the street people in Boston, meeting their physical needs in the name of Christ and telling them the good news of Jesus.

After I finished seminary I was employed by Inter-Varsity Christian Fellowship to do evangelism in the Boston area. God surrounded me with a group of committed Christians on Inter-Varsity's staff. They knocked off some of my rough edges, gave me better answers for difficult questions, and followed up a lot of people who came to the open-air meetings.

Whatever ability God has given me to answer cynics in open-air meetings is not due to me being an intellectual. I graduated from Davidson College with a grade point average of 2.9. When I told one of my preaching professors in seminary that I was going to do evangelism with Inter-Varsity he laughed. When I told a former Inter-Varsity staff worker (a classmate of mine in seminary) what I was going to do, he wondered aloud if Inter-Varsity was reaching new depths of incompetence.

I am clearly not an intellectual. But I am a plodder. The issue for me every day is not, "Cliffe, are you an intellectual?" Rather the issue is, "Cliffe, will you be obedient? Will you faithfully use the resources God has given you to build the kingdom of Christ?"

Since the fall of 1979, I have traveled to campuses and to cities around the country speaking about the love of Christ. It has been both a challenge and a joy to speak out in the open air to people.

The challenge comes as I attempt to cope with hostility and disruptions. But the joy is even greater; I see people everywhere responding to God's leading by asking honest questions and listening closely to the answers I attempt to give. It is encouraging to see the Holy Spirit so active in people's lives. I want to be a tool of that Spirit in any way I can.

This book is organized around the tough questions people ask me as I preach. I have tried to group them, for convenience, by themes. I begin where many of my questioners begin, with objections to the exclusive claims of Christ and the distasteful thought of going to hell for eternity. The problem of evil, conflicts of reason and faith, and hypocrisy in the church are other common topics.

Eventually such discussions come down to the issue of authority. Who has the most authoritative answers? I believe the Bible does. But many people have doubts and ask me to defend its integrity and historicity.

But many of these questions are often mind games or smokescreens for people who don't want to change their lifestyles. They want to keep on sleeping around or getting high every weekend. They realize that Christ's claims on our lives demand we live differently than before. If they are honest, therefore, they will begin to ask questions about morality. Chapter eight offers concluding and summary statements of many of the topics covered in the book.

I realize, of course, that these answers are not exhaustive. But I want to point people in the right direction and show them that satisfying answers are possible. As you read, you will notice some overlap among my answers too. This is because I want my answers to be well-rounded while not being too repetitious. But for me, the cross of Christ is always central. So you will find it mentioned many times. The last chapter gives a few of the lessons I have learned as I have witnessed around the country.

This book has evolved in several steps. First, some years ago, Leighton Ford encouraged me to write down my answers to questions people ask me. Second, more and more Christians who have heard me preach have expressed a desire to have these responses in written form.

I have also wanted some follow-up material for Christians to use after I leave a city or college. I hope this book will help Christians communicate with friends who are not believers. In these pages I want people to see that the gospel can stand on its own in the marketplace.

Another purpose for this book is to give some degree of credibility and substance to my ministry since open-air preachers do not have the greatest reputations. Most people assume I am a hell-fire and brimstone evangelist who waves a Bible and condemns people with King James English. Most Christians are embarrassed by such preachers. Those who are not Christians at best find it a source of amusement and entertainment and at worst a source of irritation or hatred. In any case open-air preaching is not considered something to be taken seriously.

Those who prepare for my visits therefore have sometimes had trouble convincing local pastors and other Christian leaders that my ministry is a serious one. I hope this book will at least partially do that.

But there are other far more personal reasons why I am writing this book. I am deeply motivated by my love for Christ. I want people who are not Christians to come to know Jesus Christ or want to learn more about him. The deepest desire of my heart is to see that his name is glorified and made known to more and more people.

I have seen the way sin has hurt my family, myself and those who are close to me. I want to be sensitive and patient when people fail morally, the same way I would want them to be sensitive when I fail. But my anguish over sin compels me to travel and preach the hope of Jesus Christ to a generation that is groping for answers. As I travel I see and hear the stories of people whose lives have been broken by sin. I see the desperation in the faces of those whose loneliness will either drive them to suicide or to Jesus Christ. With as much strength as God gives me and as much time as God allows me, I want to continue preaching the gospel.

I am not an expert apologist or a scholar. I don't pretend to be. I only know that I am a rebel against God who has been forgiven and who preaches God's forgiveness. In spite of the parents God has given me, the wife God has given me, and the wonderful opportunities I've been given, I still choose to rebel against God and, for whatever reason, he still chooses to use me. I am determined to struggle to allow Christ to love people through my words and actions.

One

Aren't There Many Ways to God?

Whenever I do *open-air preaching, I follow a similar* format. First, I take about seven to ten minutes to make my opening remarks. I state who I am, why I have come to speak and explain the basics of my own walk with Jesus Christ. I tell why I believe Jesus is not only the way to personal salvation but also why he gives us abundant life now.

Obviously, in the few minutes I have I cannot go into great detail. In fact, it is better for me to be brief so too many people don't wander away because they are bored or too busy to hang around. So after a short talk on an issue from a biblical perspective, I encourage people to ask questions or make comments whether they agree or disagree with what I've said.

One of the topics that often strikes my listeners is the exclusive claims of Christianity. In an age of relativism, people are quite uncomfortable when you say you have the absolute truth. In an era when people want to think that their view of what is right and what is wrong is as good as anyone else's, you will get a lot of disagreement if you say Jesus' view is ultimately true.

Question 1. Why do you say that Jesus Christ is the only way to God?

One person in Massachusetts objected, "It is narrow-minded to say that Jesus is the only way to God. Jesus, Muhammad, Krishna are all symbols of God. God isn't limited to Jesus Christ. All the major world religions point to the same God."

If all religions point to the same God, one would imagine that they would say basically the same things about him, at least in their essential teachings. But if we examine these religions, we find that they in fact disagree over fundamental points. The Bhagavad Gita, Upanishads and other holy books of Eastern mysticism teach that God is one. Everything is God. You are god. I am god. The tree is god. The dirt is god. The insect is god. Good is god. Evil is god. They also teach that God is impersonal, that God is an it.

Judaism, Christianity and Islam on the other hand teach that God is the Creator and that we are not part of him. Rather we were made by him. They also teach that God is holy and just. He has defined the difference between good and evil. God is seen as a personal being who has a special relationship to humanity.

But there is a sense in which Christianity is different from every other religion. All the other major world religions teach that you must get yourself together. You must pray five times a day, give alms, fast, take a pilgrimage, use a Tibetan prayer wheel, not eat certain foods, observe the sabbath, go to church or live a decent life or one of innumerable other possibilities. If you do these things, then maybe you will work your way to Nirvana or heaven or God.

Christianity is different. God tells us we will never *earn* heaven or *deserve* a right relationship with him. We simply cannot live up to God's standards. Instead, God has taken the initiative. Because of his great love for us, he came to earth as a man to rescue us from the penalty of death that our wrongdoing deserves. Jesus Christ, the Son of God, died on the cross to take the punishment you and I have earned.

He did something for us that we could not do for ourselves. He lived a perfect life. He did not deserve to die. He died as a sacrifice for you and me. He rose from the dead, is alive today and is offering us a gift—forgiveness and eternal life. No other religion can point to a moment in history and say, this is what God has done for you. No other religion tells how God has taken the initiative to save us. Religion is our attempt at finding God. Christianity is God's attempt at finding us.

Question 2. Isn't it enough to live a good life?

This question has come to me in many forms. Usually the inquiry goes something like, "Gandhi lived a great life, a moral life. He lived a much better life than you ever will. Are you telling me he's in hell just because he didn't follow Jesus Christ? I live a good life. Aren't good people going to heaven?"

My response is always simple and always the same. I do not know whether Gandhi will be in heaven or hell. The reason I have no answer is that I don't know how Gandhi responded to Christ before he was assassinated.

But there are some things I do know. Fifteen years before his untimely death, Gandhi wrote, "I must tell you in all humility that Hinduism, as I know it, entirely satisfies my soul, fills my whole being. I find a solace in the Bhagavad and Upanishads that I miss even in the Sermon on the Mount."

Just before his death, however, it's a far different Gandhi we hear. He wrote, "My days are numbered. I am not likely to live very long, perhaps a year or a little more. For the first time in 50 years I find myself in the slough of despond. All about me is darkness; I am praying for light." Jesus said, "I am the light of the world. Whoever follows me will never walk in darkness, but will have the light of life" (Jn 8:12). It is my personal prayer that Gandhi found the light of the world, Jesus Christ.

Often I will answer questions about living the good and perfect life by saying, "I agree; if you live the perfect life, you do not need to accept Christ. You have done nothing to disobey him, so you have no need of forgiveness. Congratulations."

I'm not trying to be facetious when I respond this way. I'm trying to say, as kindly as I can, that no one can short-circuit God. None of us have lived a good and perfect life, as God defines those words. In Mark 12:30-31 Jesus explains what he means by the "good life." "Love the Lord your God with all your heart and with all your soul and with all your mind and with all your strength. Love your neighbor as yourself."

That's all we have to do to make it to heaven. If we can accomplish it, without slippage, without failure, then we can attain salvation on our own.

For those who continue to insist that all it requires to attain heavenly status is a good set of moral credentials, I tell a well-known story of the Scriptures, the story of the rich young man found in Matthew 19:16-21.

Here was a man who had everything—money, possessions, prestige and respect—and he had acquired them honestly, without deceit. One day this young man approached Jesus with the question, "Teacher, what good thing must I do to get eternal life?"

Jesus' answer must have surprised the young man: "Why do you ask me about what is good? There is only One who is good." Right away Jesus challenges our definition of *good.* Only God has the right to that title. Kind of sobering, isn't it? Especially when many claim that all it takes is a "good" life to attain our salvation. But the only perfect "good" that exists, according to Jesus, is the perfection found in God.

Christ went on from there. He told the young man, "Obey the commandments . . . 'Do not murder; do not commit

21

adultery, do not steal, do not give false testimony, honor your father and mother, and love your neighbor as yourself.' "

The young man must have thought, "Hey, this is a piece of cake. I've done all of this." So he replies, "All these I have kept."

Jesus wasn't finished though. "If you want to be perfect, go, sell your possessions, and give to the poor. Then come, follow me."

When Jesus said that, the young man's demeanor changed immediately. He put his head down and walked away. Sadness filled his heart. Jesus had touched him at the center of who he was. Although this young man may have been blameless in his personal life and in his business life, he was still busy serving another God—money. He didn't realize that goodness, as defined by God, applies to our attitudes as well as to our actions.

This all comes down to one basic question: If it's possible for you and me to attain salvation by simply living a good life, why was it necessary for Jesus to endure the excruciating agony of the cross? Why didn't he simply lay down a few guidelines, tell us to do our best, and then ascend into heaven? Why? Because Jesus knew it would take more than guidelines to redeem us. He knew we could not make it on our own, that we could not work our way to God.

But God has worked his way to us in Jesus Christ. The punishment we deserve, justly deserve, was suffered by him. The only way we can be "good" is if we partake of Jesus' goodness, which, fortunately, he wants us to have.

Question 3. Will saying a little prayer save even a very evil person?

Once a young man asked me, "If a man lives a horrible life—if he murders, steals and rapes—then, just before his death he prays a little prayer and tells Jesus he's sorry . . . you mean to tell me that that man will go to heaven? What about me? I live a decent life, but I've never accepted Jesus. You mean to tell me I won't go to heaven?"

A "little prayer" cannot save anybody. Only God can save us, and only God knows when someone truly turns to him. When answering such a question, we should be careful not to speculate about what might constitute a "legitimate" conversion. Rather, we should simply say exactly what we know from Scripture.

One thing we know is that Scripture is filled with warnings about dealing superficially with the promises of Jesus Christ. Jesus said, "Not everyone who says to me, 'Lord, Lord,' will enter the kingdom of heaven, but only he who does the will of my father who is in heaven. Many will say to me on that day, 'Lord, Lord, did we not prophesy in your name, and in your name drive out demons and perform many miracles?' Then I will tell them plainly, 'I never knew you. Away from me, you evildoers!' " (Mt 7:21-23). It is only genuine sorrow for our past that will be acceptable to Christ. And only he is capable of discerning that.

We know that Jesus commanded us to "repent and believe" (Mk 1:15). *Repent* may seem like an archaic word. But it's what happens when you want to change yourself. It means being willing to say you have done wrong in the past, that you now regret it and that you want to live differently.

Suppose I were to haul back and slap you in the face and immediately say, "Oh, I'm terribly sorry. I've made an awful mistake. Will you please forgive me?"

You might be very gracious and say, "Yes, Cliffe. Certainly I forgive you." But if I haul back and slap you again, you know I'm a flaming hypocrite. If I had genuinely regretted slapping you in the face, I would have made a more serious attempt to change my behavior. Does this mean we will live perfect lives after we become Christians? Not at all. It means we must truly desire to be different and be willing to do whatever we can to be different.

In 2 Corinthians 7:10-11 Paul writes, "Godly sorrow brings repentance that leads to salvation and leaves no regret, but worldly sorrow brings death. See what this godly sorrow has produced in you: what earnestness, what eagerness to clear yourselves, what indignation, what alarm, what longing, what concern, what readiness to see justice done." Godly sorrow means I am highly motivated to correct the wrong that I've done in the past. It means I am upset at wrongdoing. I am alarmed when I see evil. It means I am ready to change.

In addition to repentance, Jesus also called for belief. Today a lot of people think this means to give intellectual assent to certain facts. But James 2:19 makes it clear that this is not sufficient. "You believe that there is one God. Good! Even the demons believe that—and shudder." Belief in God apparently doesn't do evil spirits any good. More is needed.

Belief is an act of the will. It is a decision to trust, to commit one's life. To commit our lives to Christ is to believe in him and in all that he said and commanded. To believe means to trust Christ with your life. Loyalty and obedience to Christ are also important parts of belief in him. Even though we may not be able to judge the sincerity of others, we know that repentance and belief are what Jesus looks for in us.

There is one particular incident in Scripture (I guess you could call it a deathbed or foxhole conversion) in which Christ offers salvation to someone who has led a criminal life and at the last moment repents. When Jesus was hanging on the cross, two thieves were crucified on either side of him. One thief looked at Jesus and said, "Aren't you the Christ? Save yourself and us!"

But the second thief cut him off, "Don't you fear God . . . since you are under the same sentence? We are being punished justly for we are getting what our deeds deserve. But this man has done nothing wrong." Then he said, "Jesus, remember me when you come into your kingdom."

Jesus answered him, "I tell you the truth, today you will be with me in paradise" (Lk 23:39-43). Jesus was able to tell that this man repented genuinely. But it is up to Christ to discern that, not us.

The idea that God would save someone who repents at the last minute just doesn't seem fair to us. This was the challenge behind the young man's question. In Matthew 20:1-16 Jesus tells a parable that addresses this issue directly. He describes a vineyard owner who hires laborers for his field. He hired some workers to come in the morning and offered to pay them one denarius for their work. Later he hired others who came later in the morning, and still others who came in the early and late afternoon. In fact, the last group was hired only one hour before quitting time. The owner contracted with each of them for one denarius for the day's work.

When the time came to collect their wages, those workers who had been in the fields since the beginning of the day complained that they were getting the same amount as those who had worked only an hour. They protested that this was unfair. "Not so," said the owner. "You contracted with me for a specific amount, and I honored my contract with you."

If God gave us what we deserved, we would all be in trouble. In fact, we would all be dead. We should be thankful that Jesus was willing to pay the penalty in our place. God does not limit his love and mercy to those who are ethically superior. If this is unfair, then we should get down on our knees and praise God that he is more loving than fair.

Question 4. Does it matter what you believe as long as you are sincere?

Many people have said to me, "It doesn't matter what you believe just as long as you are sincere." This is based on the popular belief that there are no moral absolutes. Everything is relative. Neither are there religious absolutes. It is all subjective experience. Albert Einstein's general theory of relativity was meant to apply to physical properties. Unfortunately people have applied it to every area of life. Tolerance has become the queen of virtues. It is the only virtue that has escaped the corroding cynicism that characterizes too many of us. There are several reasons for this.

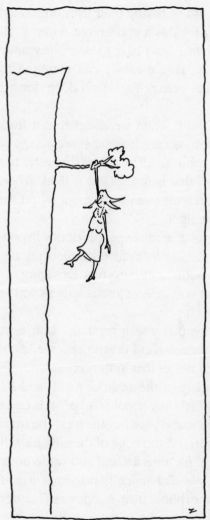

PATRICIA
BEGINS
TO SUSPECT THAT
HER SINCERITY
IS NOT GOING
TO HELP MUCH
IN HER PRESENT
SITUATION.

First, it sounds enlightened and open-minded to say that everyone will get the prize, that everyone will win the race, that all roads lead to the top of the mountain. It has a generous, benevolent feel to it.

Second, people are afraid of having their lives unmasked by the truth. Tolerance provides a convenient cover. If all religions are the same, then I don't have to take Christianity seriously. I can ignore it. That means I can continue to ignore the dark side of my personality which deep down I know is there.

We are scared of the truth. When we compare our lives to what Christ has revealed, we see how far short we fall of true goodness. We are confronted by the dishonesty, the self-centeredness, the evil that is in us. God is light. When that light shines on us it reveals everything about us. So we tend to run away from the light.

Third, tolerance is popular because people abhor hypocrisy. But this is an overreaction to insincerity. Sincerity becomes so important that nothing else matters. By saying, "It really doesn't matter what you believe just as long as you're sincere," we throw out truth.

Jesus Christ attacked hypocrisy as a great sin, but Jesus clearly taught that truth matters. And down deep we know that to be true. Reality teaches us that truth is critical.

If a blind man is standing at the edge of a cliff and he turns to you and asks, "Which way should I step?" it is cruel if you respond, "It doesn't matter; just be sincere." The truth is that if the blind man steps off the edge of the cliff, he will plunge to his death. But if he turns around and walks away from the edge, he will live. Tolerance is no virtue if you ignore reality and tell the blind man it does not matter where he steps, just as long as he is sincere. Rather, the virtue lies in telling the truth. "You are on a cliff!"

In medicine, truth is vital. It would be cruel (should we say evil?) if a doctor looked a patient in the face and said, "You have a malignant tumor that is spreading throughout your body. It really doesn't matter though. You can either go home and allow the tumor to continue to consume your body, or else you can allow me to surgically remove it. Either way is fine. Just be sincere. Just be a nice guy and everything will turn out all right."

The doctor knows that the tumor is destroying that human life, and motivated by truth he will look into the face of the patient and say, "My friend, there is a tumor that is eating away at your body. It will end in death. But I can surgically remove it to help prolong your life. I would encourage you with everything in me to allow me to do the surgery." That is virtuous—sincerity with truth.

Jesus said, "It is not the healthy who need a doctor, but the sick. I have not come to call the righteous, but sinners" (Mk 2:17). Jesus clearly taught that we have a disease— rebellion against God. That disease ends in death and hell. Jesus Christ wants to bring real forgiveness and healing to the disease of sin. Jesus Christ offers eternal life. To display cynicism toward Jesus Christ in the face of death is to make a cataclysmic mistake.

Suppose a student didn't study for an exam. Instead she just went into the test and allowed her inner being to flow out all over her exam paper. Then when she received the result she went to her professor and said, "Professor, how could you flunk me? I really expressed the way I felt on this exam. I was honest. I was sincere."

The professor will look her in the face and say, "You were honestly wrong. You were sincerely mistaken. You flunk."

Truth matters when you go take a test. The day of judgment will be the final exam when you and I will stand
before God and have to give an account for all of our actions, all of our words, all of our thoughts. And the question
is, Are you ready for that final exam?

But even if God would judge us on our sincerity, we
would be on dangerous ground. Which one of us can genuinely say, "I have been completely sincere. I have never
doubted. I have never had mixed or tarnished motives"?
None of us. All of us in some way have been twisted and
false. But Jesus Christ loves us even with our twisted motives, and he wants to live in us, to begin to change our
motives. Jesus Christ wants to change our insincerity into
sincere desires. The question is, Will we allow him to come
in? Will we allow him to begin to straighten our twisted
selves? Will we allow him to purify what is corrupt? He'll do
it if we ask him.

Question 5. Won't heaven be boring?

Some people don't think spending eternity in heaven is a
very attractive prospect. They think it will be sitting on a
cloud strumming a harp forever. If that is heaven, I'm quite
sure I don't want to go. I don't enjoy sitting on clouds and
I'm not a harp player either. But Jesus said, "This is eternal
life: that they may know you, the only true God, and Jesus
Christ, whom you have sent" (Jn 17:3)

In heaven the deep love relationship we began in this life

with the living God and with others will be fulfilled. My relationships with people and my relationship with God brings me the most joy, fulfillment and satisfaction now. Heaven will be an eternal love relationship with the living God and with other created beings. There is no more exciting place that a human being could possibly be. That is what all of us are striving for now—deep, open, honest relationships of love with other people.

Today we all have questions that drill at our hearts and our minds. I know I've got a string of questions for God that I'm looking forward to having answered. And I can hardly wait until I can see God face to face in an intimate relationship and talk these over with him for as long as I want.

Jesus also taught that in heaven we would have new bodies, bodies like his resurrection body. He promised each one of us a body that would not decay, that would not grow old, that would not die. I am looking forward to that kind of body! It means that my friends who were born with brain damage or with birth defects, who have severe diseases, who have died and whose bodies are rotting in the ground—all my friends who have trusted Christ are going to have new bodies. They will have bodies without birth defects or disease that will last an eternity. I'm looking forward to that.

Eastern mysticism teaches that we are to work toward Nirvana, a state of absolute blessedness reached by denying our individuality, our unique personality, our very self.

But Jesus Christ teaches that our unique personalities are valuable and significant. When he returns there will be a resurrection, and he will give each of us a unique body. My friends will be able to recognize me. I will be able to recognize them. We are not going to become one with pure spirit. We're not going to be a drop added to the ocean of nothingness. We will retain our individuality and personality and significance.

Another reason for looking forward to heaven is because in this world there are all types of problems: lust, greed, racism, sexism, terrorism, chauvinism. But in heaven, none of these will exist. In heaven there will be no more war, famine, suffering, disease or evil. In heaven there will be eternal peace. When Jesus Christ returns in power and great glory, he will forcefully put down all evil, all oppression, all exploitation, and he will destroy death. Today we have wars. Today we have a crime rate that's soaring. But in heaven there will be no more wars. In heaven there will be no more crime. There will be eternal peace in the presence of the living God.

Most people think praising God for eternity will be boring because they imagine themselves sitting around singing hymns day in and day out. Well you don't have to sit around to praise God. You can praise God by serving him in a myriad of different ways, some of which entail being very active. In fact, the Bible teaches that in heaven we will be using our time, our energies, our gifts and abilities to serve God and to serve each other. There will be much work to do, and it will be work that will be unhindered by evil, by laziness, by apathy, by indifference. In heaven we will know the excitement of worshiping God and working and playing with each other in perfect harmony.

There's one thing about praise that I find fascinating. I am deeply in love with my wife. When those feelings of love begin to well up within me they flow out in the form of praise. When I genuinely praise my wife, that is the zenith of my love experience with her. In heaven we will be so

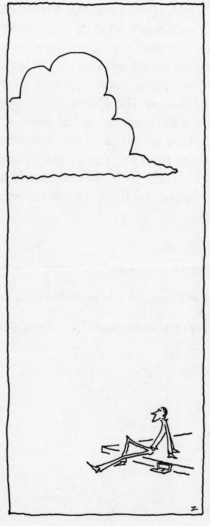

ARNOLD DECIDES
THAT EVEN IF
HEAVEN'S BORING,
IT PROBABLY
BEATS MILWAUKEE.

filled with love for God that it will flow out of us constantly in the form of praise and thanksgiving to him.

No matter how glorious and fulfilling we imagine heaven to be, the reality will be much greater. The apostle John was caught up in a vision of heaven. Human language failed him. He writes about a city of gold surrounded by walls decorated with precious stones. The gates on the walls are made of pearls. Inside the city the streets are paved with gold, transparent like glass. The apostle John is totally overwhelmed by the vision of heaven. The apostle Paul writes concerning heaven, "No eye has seen, no ear has heard, no mind has conceived what God has prepared for those who love him" (1 Cor 2:9). There is no way that you or I living within the limits of space and time could ever imagine how fantastic heaven will be. But of one thing we can be sure, heaven will not be boring.

Suggested Reading
Peter Kreeft. *Heaven: The Heart's Deepest Longing.* San Francisco: Harper & Row, 1980.
Stephen Neill. *Christian Faith and Other Faiths.* Downers Grove, Ill.: InterVarsity Press, 1984.
Lesslie Newbigin. *The Finality of Christ.* Richmond, Va.: John Knox, 1969.

Two

Does God Really Send People to Hell?

The idea of *hell is a very uncomfortable one. We don't* like the notion of spending eternity in a place of intense suffering. And besides, in our materialistic age, hell seems somehow superstitious. The image of demons with tails and pitchforks hurling people into flaming furnaces seems a bit ridiculous to our sophisticated, high-tech sensibilities. It's even a comic image used often in cartoons and jokes. So we tend to dismiss it with a laugh.

So when I tell people that they are responsible for making

a decision that will not only affect their life now but how they will spend eternity, questions begin to pop. Truth may not be popular. But a lack of popularity doesn't make it any less true. A vote against the law of gravity would not send us floating off into space. We'd still be grounded on good old planet Earth. Likewise, the fact that most people don't believe in hell doesn't mean they won't end up there.

I said earlier that I hate sin and its effects on people. I care enough to give them the bad news (you are condemned), because the good news is so vital. I don't want the people I meet to be separated from God for eternity. So I tell them about hell. I don't try to scare people into the kingdom. But hell is part of the whole message of the Bible, and so I don't hide it from those I talk to.

Question 6. Is there really going to be a hell?

From the East Coast to the West Coast I am consistently asked, "Do you believe there is really going to be a hell?"

I have never been to hell. It is not personal experience that tells me hell exists. I believe there will be a hell because Jesus Christ clearly taught there would be. I know that Jesus is trustworthy, that he is not a liar. Jesus spoke more about hell than any other writer in the whole Bible.

Jesus said, for example, "If your right eye causes you to sin, gouge it out and throw it away. It is better for you to lose one part of your body than for your whole body to be thrown into hell" (Mt 5:29). He also said, "The Son of Man will send out his angels, and they will weed out of his kingdom everything that causes sin and all who do evil. They will throw them into the fiery furnace, where there will be weeping and gnashing of teeth" (Mt 13:41-42).

In Luke 16:19-31 Jesus told a story about a rich man who had the finest of clothes, was in good health and feasted sumptuously every day. Daily a beggar named Lazarus lay at the foot of the table. He was a pitiful sight. His body was covered with sores and the dogs would lick the sores through his tattered clothing. But Lazarus longed to grab the crumbs as they fell from the rich man's table and stuff them into his mouth because he was hungry.

Eventually both men died. The rich man went to hell. The poor man went to heaven. In hell, where the rich man was in torment, he looked up and saw poor Lazarus at the side of father Abraham in heaven. So the rich man called out, "Father Abraham, have pity on me and send Lazarus to dip the tip of his finger in water and cool my tongue, because I am in agony in this fire."

But Abraham replied, "Son, remember that in your lifetime you received your good things while Lazarus received bad things, but now he is comforted here and you are in agony. And besides all this, between us and you a great chasm has been fixed, so that those who want to go from here to you cannot, nor can anyone cross over from there to us."

When the rich man found himself in hell, he had to beg for a drop of cold water. But unfortunately, there was a huge gulf separating heaven from hell. No one could cross over from one to the other.

There is an awful finality to hell. There is no possibility of working one's way from hell to heaven. This life is the time that you and I have to decide where we will spend eternity. Life is not a silly game. Life is for keeps.

A lot of people say, "I'm looking forward to going to hell. That's where all my buddies will be. We'll have a party. We'll have a great time." That is only wishful thinking. In hell there will be no partying. There will be no fun and games. There will be eternal darkness, eternal separation from God and from others. Eternal aloneness.

In Jesus' story the rich man was a decent, law-abiding citizen. He allowed the beggar to lie beside his dining table. He gave the beggar more than most people did. He gave him his crumbs. But the rich man stuffed his mouth with food and then looked into the face of the starving man and was totally unmoved. Although the rich man had many things, he didn't have a heart.

We are just like the rich man in Jesus' story. He tried to live a good life and so do we. But the rich man was blind to his own apathy and lack of love. In the same way we have been blind to our wrongdoing. We have found it difficult to believe, to trust, to have faith. But today Jesus Christ offers forgiveness and eternal life if we will put our faith in him.

Question 7. How could a loving God send people to hell?

"If God cares about us and is so loving, how can he possibly send anyone to hell?" That's what one professor asked me. He added, "Isn't that inconsistent?"

Don't we all get angry when we hear about some blatant

evil? Don't reports of child abuse or murders by terrorists get us upset? And isn't there a sense that we should be upset over such things, that not caring or being pleased about such incidents would be wrong? Well, in a way, that is something like what God feels when he sees evil in the world. But his indignation is multiplied many times. Indeed it is of an entirely different magnitude.

God is just, holy and morally perfect. We all stand guilty before God because we fall far short of his perfection. But the Bible also reveals that God is loving and merciful. He has provided a way to escape the condemnation we deserve. He has sent his Son to die for us.

Two close friends graduated from college in Australia. One became a judge and the other a banker. One day the banker was arrested for embezzlement of one million dollars. He was to be tried before his friend. There was great speculation in the press. Would the judge throw the book at his buddy, proving what a just judge he was? Or would he let his friend off free? The courtroom was packed. The jury deliberated. They delivered the verdict—guilty. The judge then gave the sentence. He leveled the harshest fine possible against his friend.

The crowd gasped in amazement. But then everyone watched in wonder as the judge stood, took off his robe, walked around the bar and extended his hand to his friend. He said, "I have sold my house, taken all my savings out of my account. I have paid the fine I just leveled against you."

The judge was just and the judge was loving. Justice was honored. But friendship was honored too. And all in the one act of paying the fine. That is how it works with Christ's death on the cross. In one act both justice and love are found.

God cannot turn his back on sin. He cannot ignore it. But the penalty for our sin was paid by his Son's death. And he cannot ignore that either. All he asks us to do is accept it. God carries out perfect judgment and perfect compassion. It's his nature, and he cannot violate it. If we accept God's offer of forgiveness and love through Jesus Christ, God's perfect compassion will grant it. If we do not accept it, then God's perfect justice has no choice but to hold us account-able for the wrong we've done. And he has made clear that the penalty is eternal death in hell.

God is not merely a doddering old grandfather with a white beard who sits on a throne in the sky and smiles as he lets everyone pass by. He's not hanging around saying, "Well, Hitler, you murdered a few folks at Dachau, Buchen-wald and Auschwitz, but I understand you're simply a prod-uct of your environment. I'm all-forgiving; enter heaven."

That's not being loving—that's being amoral. Instead of asking, "How could a caring God allow a hell to exist?" the question ought to be, "How could a caring God *not* allow a hell to exist?"

In California a woman asked, "Do you mean to say that if I reject Jesus Christ I will go to hell?"

I said, "The Bible clearly teaches that you and I have rebelled against God. The penalty for that rebellion is hell. The good news is that Jesus Christ died to pay the penalty of hell we deserve. But we have to make our own decision to ask Christ for forgiveness, to put our faith in him and to receive the gift of eternal life.

"If we reject Christ we are rejecting God's offer of forgive-ness. On the day of judgment God will hold us accountable for the wrong we have done and we will go to hell."

The woman turned around and walked away from the

crowd. A short distance from the crowd she was met by a Christian woman who communicated simply and powerfully that that young lady needed to receive Christ. She made that decision.

Question 8. Should I accept Jesus just so I won't go to hell?

After answering how God could create hell, there are still those who ask, "So, the reason I should accept your Jesus is so I won't go to hell?" C. S. Lewis thought it was amazing that God would accept people simply for the lousy reason that they don't want to go to hell.

This statement by Lewis points directly to the depth of God's love for us and patience with us. Avoiding hell is not the reason people should place their trust in Christ. There are several other far more important reasons: First, he is the truth, historically and spiritually. Second, we should receive Christ so that we can live out the purpose for which we were created—fellowship with the living God.

Another reason people accept Christ is because they are, as Lewis also said, "surprised by joy." They never knew that such an unconditional love as Christ's existed.

Whenever I speak to students I want that surprise to hit them. I want that to be the reason they accept Jesus Christ. I don't want to scare anyone into the kingdom of God by dangling them over the pit of hell.

Question 9. Are those who have never heard about Christ going to hell?

It is quite common for people to ask about the "heathen in Africa" or others who never had an opportunity to hear the gospel. And it is quite legitimate to ask how God will judge such people. Frankly, however, I do not know how God will judge those who have never heard of Christ. But I do know five things that help us understand the issue.

First, God is just. He will judge each person uniquely and fairly. God is far more just than you or I could ever hope to be. On the day of judgment justice shall be given each person by God.

Second, nobody is going to hell because they haven't heard about Christ. Nobody is going to hell because of a lack of knowledge or a low IQ. The only reason people are going to hell is because all life long they have told God that they can live just fine without him. On the judgment day God will say, "Based on your own decision to live life separately from me, you will spend eternity separate from me." That's hell. God will not violate our will. If all life long we have said, "My will be done," then on the day of judgment God will say to you, "your will be done for eternity." G. K. Chesterton put it this way: "Hell is God's great compliment to the reality of human freedom and the dignity of human choice."

Third, there will be many people in heaven who lived before Jesus who never heard his name. Hebrews 11 clearly says that those who lived before Christ and who put their faith in God will be in heaven. Abraham, Moses and Rahab the Jericho prostitute are just a few of those who responded to the light God gave them. They understood they were in need. They trusted in the Lord. The result of their faith was obedience. They will be in heaven.

Next, the only reason anyone will be in heaven is because Jesus bled and died on the cross to pay the penalty for human sin. Nobody will be in heaven because they lived a good life or because they were sincere. Rather they will receive eternal life as a result of God's good gift to them in Christ.

Finally, those who have heard about Christ will be held accountable for how they responded to him. To reject Christ is to reject God's offer of forgiveness and eternal life. To choose not to decide about Jesus is to reject him. Love demands a choice. To remain apathetic in the face of love is to mock the One who loves. A loving God invites us to come to him.

Question 10. Doesn't the Old Testament talk about a God of wrath and the New Testament talk about a God of love?

A question that comes up often in my discussions involves the portrayal of God in the Old and the New Testaments. A student at Northwestern University in Evanston, Illinois, asked, "the God of the Old Testament is a God of wrath, while the God of the New Testament is a God of love. How do you explain this contradiction?"

The fact is that both the Old and New Testaments reveal that God is a God of love. He is holy and loving. Both testaments also reveal that he is a God of judgment and wrath.

In the Old Testament, God used prophets such as Amos, Jeremiah, Isaiah and Micah to issue his warnings. God had brought his chosen people, Israel, out of bondage in Egypt. He had brought them to a new and a flourishing land. Yet, as is so often true with us, Israel responded to her redeemer by saying, "Nice work, but what have you done for me lately?"

God sent his prophets to warn his people that they were really testing his patience. Not only were they openly rebellious, they seemed to be proud of it. Scripture uses a beautiful word for this kind of attitude: *stiffnecked.*

As well as being a record of God's wrath and pronouncement of judgment against his people, the Old Testament is also a document of promise and hope. The fifty-third chapter of Isaiah is a prophetic metaphor about the suffering servant who would be beaten, bruised and crushed to pay the penalty for human sin and our rebellion against God.

Surely he took up our infirmities
 and carried our sorrows,
yet we considered him stricken by God,
 smitten by him, and afflicted.
But he was pierced for our transgressions,
 he was crushed for our iniquities;
the punishment that brought us peace was upon him,
 and by his wounds we are healed. (Is 53:4-6)

Even Jeremiah, the weeping prophet, had a word of solace. He reveals God's lament, "I have loved you with an everlasting love, I have drawn you with loving-kindness." He makes a promise to the people of Israel who were being taken into exile as slaves because of their sins:

See, I will bring them from the land of the north,
and gather them from the ends of the earth.
Among them will be the blind and the lame,
expectant mothers and women in labor;
a great throng will return.
They will come with weeping;
they will pray as I bring them back.
I will lead them beside streams of water
on a level path where they will not stumble.
(Jer 31:8-9)

This supposed contradiction between the Old and New Testaments also loses credibility when we come to the book of the Old Testament prophet Hosea. It is one of the most compelling stories of love and redemption in the entire biblical record.

Hosea was married to a woman named Gomer. Each night as they lay in their bed, they would hear distant music from the center of town come wafting in through the windows. Gomer would get up and leave her husband, who was an elderly man, and walk the streets searching for younger, stronger, more virile men. When she found one, she would stay the night with him.

Every morning Hosea would get up and follow the same routine. He'd walk the streets of the city searching for his wife. He would usually find her bruised and lying in the gutter. He would reach out to her to lift her up, but she would shrink back—she didn't even recognize her husband through the haze of the previous evening.

Hosea would bring her home, wash her wounds and bandage her. But every night when the music started up, Gomer would be gone again, out on the streets selling herself to the highest bidder.

Gomer's lovers suddenly decided they had had enough of her. She was so bruised and battered that she didn't serve their purposes anymore. They needed to move on and exploit someone else. So they offered her up to the highest bidder at the slave market.

I imagine that many of us would have left Gomer to her own devices by this time. We would have stoically and self-righteously pronounced, "I've done all I'm going to do. She made her bed with whoever she wanted. Now let her sleep in it."

Hosea, though, was made out of different material. The love he felt for Gomer was stronger than any bitterness or anger he might have felt. He went back to the slave market to buy back his wife. Hosea outbid the other men and bought Gomer back. As they were walking home, he said to her, "Gomer, my love for you is still the same. I bought you back at a very high price. From this day forth you will live with me as my wife, and be faithful. You will no longer play the prostitute."

God was teaching Israel a lesson as well as Hosea. God was saying, "Hosea, you know the pain you've experienced over your wife's unfaithfulness. That's the same pain I experience. People who I have created to love me have turned their backs and gone after idols. I hurt because of the unfaithfulness of my people. And at great cost I intend to pursue them and to buy them back from the slave market."

So the Old Testament is not simply a document of wrath.

It resounds with the loving calls of a holy God for his wayward children. Remarkably, the New Testament reveals God in all his wrath and indignation. There are many recorded incidents in which Jesus looks squarely into the faces of the religious hypocrites and says, "How will you escape being condemned to hell?" Many people have this "gentle Jesus, meek and mild" image of the Savior. Nothing could be further from the truth. In all of Scripture, there was no one who talked about hell more than Jesus Christ.

And the bloodiest book of all of Scripture is not found in the Old Testament. It is found in the New Testament in the book of Revelation. The blood flows deeper and thicker in that book than anywhere else in Scripture.

The New Testament also speaks very clearly about God's judgment. Jesus promised that one day he would return. But this return would be different than his first coming. This time he will not be coming as an infant, but as the returning judge who will bring his justice to all the earth.

Suggested Reading

Norman Anderson. *Christianity and World Religions,* 2nd ed. Downers Grove, Ill.: InterVarsity Press, 1984.

C. S. Lewis. *The Great Divorce.* New York: Macmillan, 1978.

Three

Why Is There
So Much Evil
In the World?

When anyone *starts telling people about Jesus, it doesn't* take long before questions about God's goodness and the world's evils begin to arise. And this is not surprising. On the one hand we preach about God's great love for us in sending Christ and meeting our needs and answering our prayers. On the other hand the news media are full of reports of wars, starvation, crime, corruption, murder and terrorism. How do we reconcile these two? How can we defend God as a God of love when so much evil exists? That is the focus of the questions in this chapter.

Question 11. Why do innocent people suffer?

For thousands of years philosophers and theologians have struggled with the classical problem of why an all-loving and all-powerful God would allow evil to exist. In all that time they have never come up with a complete answer.

Neither will I be able to answer that question completely. But as Christians we must think about this issue and, I think, we can approach an answer.

First, some have tried to solve the problem of evil by simply saying God doesn't exist. Evil and good are simply two aspects of reality that war against one another. But if there is no God, there is no Creator to create the ultimate values of good and evil. And if there is no good and evil, the problem of suffering is gone too. If God does not exist, our moral indignation over what we think is wrong is simply personal prejudice, subjective feeling. Bertrand Russell said, "There is no God, therefore there is no good and evil." But deep within us something cries out against the murder of innocent people, the abuse of children, the rape of women. We know these are wrong because our consciences rise up against them.

The conscience is actually a gift from the Creator who is just and who defines good and evil. The fact that a conscience exists indicates, therefore, that there is a conscience-giver. For without a conscience-giver, without God, we

ED USES HIS
INNATE SENSE
OF RIGHT AND
WRONG TO
DECIDE BETWEEN
BECOMING A
PROFESSIONAL
BOWLER OR AN
INTERNATIONAL
TERRORIST.

couldn't tell what is good and what isn't. In fact, just before Bertrand Russell died, he said, "To love is good. To hate is evil." Isn't it amazing that we as human beings have an innate ability and desire to distinguish between good and evil, right and wrong?

Don't make the mistake of using moral indignation as an argument against God's existence. For if there is no God, there is no authority to define what is absolutely right and what is abolutely wrong. Suddenly the individual or society becomes the authority. Good quickly becomes that which is expedient, easiest to do, or economically beneficial.

One society says racism or a reign of terror is best for the nation. Another society concludes that equality and freedom are just values. If there is no God to define justice and morality, each society is correct for itself. Everything is relative.

In Marcel Proust's *Remembrance of Things Past,* a lady named Oriane must decide how to spend an evening. She can either sit by the bed of a dying man or go to dine in town. She has no foundation for morality. There is no choice between good and evil. The choice is simply between what she wants to do and what she doesn't want to do. She chooses to go to dine in town because it takes less effort. There is a type of logic to her decision. She has limited resources in a short life. Why waste them on a dying man? Why not seize the evening for herself?

Jesus Christ steps into this cruel cycle of relativity and points to the values of love and compassion created by God to be enjoyed by men and women. Christ delivers us from the superficiality of a life of expediency and ushers us into a life committed to justice and truth. Deep within each one of us are the fragments of a conscience that long to embrace

51

the values God created for us to enjoy.

Second, Genesis 1 clearly communicates that when God created, all his creation was very good. God did not create evil, suffering or death. He created us to enjoy himself, each other, and to celebrate his gift of life. Genesis 3 is the tragic record of how man and woman chose to reject God. The Bible, history books and the morning newspaper record how an unmeasurable amount of evil has followed in the wake of human rebellion against God. The vast majority of this carnage is a direct result of human choice.

A student at the University of North Carolina protested, "Where is God in Ethiopia? Does he not hear the screams of babies as they starve to death? Why has God done this?"

I responded, "How can you blame God for starving babies in Ethiopia when the best-selling books in the United States are on dieting, on how to take the extra fat off? It is not God's fault that people are starving today. The earth produces enough food right now to give every person 3,000 calories a day. The problem is that some of us hoard for ourselves so that others of us go to bed starving at night. It is a cop-out to blame God for human irresponsibility. If a person gets drunk, drives his car across the median, and sends your friend to an early grave, will you blame God? Do you blame God for Hitler's seven million murders? That would be escapism. The vast majority of human evil and suffering is a direct result of human irresponsibility."

God created us to love him and each other. I deeply love my wife, Sharon. Suppose all I had to do to hear her say, "I love you, Cliffe," was to push a button in her back and out it would come. That wouldn't be love. That wouldn't be a relationship. It would be a programmed response from a computer. A relationship demands love. Love requires a choice. It cannot be forced. God created us in his image. That means when God commands, we can obey or disobey.

God gave me a hand. I can use this hand to pick up a gun and shoot you or I can use this hand to feed hungry people. God gave me a mind. I can use my mind to build a bomb or to find a cure for cancer. If I blast people into oblivion and then blame God, I am an escape artist. God did not force me to travel down either path. I chose to abuse the gift of a mind that God gave me. Evil is one of the consequences of the freedom God has given us. I preach Christ because I want people to use their freedom to choose the good.

Third, in light of the fact that human beings rebelled against God and created enormous suffering, why doesn't God punish us now? C. S. Lewis said, "The question is not 'Why do the innocent suffer?' but rather 'Why don't we all suffer more?' " At the time of Noah, God judged people by sending a flood because every inclination of their thoughts was only evil all the time (Gen 6:5). God destroyed Sodom and Gomorrah because of the people's wickedness. God used the Jewish nation to judge the Canaanite nations for sacrificing their babies and indulging in temple prostitution. Then God used the Assyrian and Babylonian nations to judge the Jewish nation for its idolatry.

When some people told Jesus about those whose blood Pilate had mixed with their sacrifices and about the eighteen who died when the tower of Siloam fell on them, Jesus replied, "Do you think these Galileans were worse sinners than all the other Galileans because they suffered this way? I tell you, no! But unless you repent, you too will all perish" (Lk 13:1-5).

Jesus promised to return and to justly judge the peoples

of the earth. Christ will destroy sin, evil and injustice when he comes in power and great glory. Why doesn't God end all evil now? Why doesn't Christ end human history now? The Bible reveals, "The Lord . . . is patient with you, not wanting anyone to perish, but everyone to come to repentance" (2 Pet 3:9). I do not know when or why God chooses to judge and punish people today. But I do know that he is patiently waiting for us to humble ourselves before him and to receive his forgiveness and eternal life. Now is the time to choose. When he returns, judgment will begin.

Fourth, at the University of Maine a young man painfully asked, "My younger sister fell on the concrete next to a pool. She broke some bones. When she was just about healed, she fell again and broke some more bones. Her bones were nearly mended when she stumbled and broke another bone. What's the story? Is God playing a sadistic game with my little sister?"

Babies are born with multiple birth defects. Genetic disorders plague many of us. An earthquake levels a city, and thousands lose their lives in the rubble. The Bible teaches that there is not always a one-to-one correspondence between sin and suffering. When we human beings told God to shove off, he partially honored our request. Nature began to revolt. The earth was cursed. Genetic breakdown and disease began. Pain and death became part of the human experience. The good creation was marred. We live in an unjust world. We are born into a world made chaotic and unfair by a humanity in revolt against its Creator.

Fifth, the book of Job reveals there is a personal being named Satan who works to bring pain, disaster and death into the lives of people. If a person suffers and is angry with God, frequently that is misplaced anger. God is the giver of life. Satan is the destroyer, the one who tears down life. Often pain is not the direct result of sin but rather the handiwork of Satan. Paul, for example, wrote to the Corinthians, "There was given me a thorn in my flesh, a messenger of Satan, to torment me" (2 Cor 12:7).

Sixth, in Jesus, God stepped into this world marred by human rebellion and the destruction of Satan. When Jesus was confronted by pain and disease, he brought healing through the use of a miracle. He did not use his supernatural power to feather his nest but rather to heal the sick and raise the dead.

Jesus commanded his followers not only to trust him in all circumstances but also to love those who bring them pain. Jesus said, "If someone strikes you on the right cheek, turn to him the other also. . . . Love your enemies and pray for those who persecute you" (Mt 5:39, 44). This type of trust in God and love for all people produces Christlike character. Paul writes, "Suffering produces perseverance; Perseverance, character" (Rom 5:3-4).

C. S. Lewis writes, "God whispers to us in our pleasures, speaks in our conscience, but shouts in our pains: it is his megaphone to rouse a deaf world." The amazing truth taught in Scripture is that God can take suffering and pain, and produce something good and beautiful. Many people have told me how God used pain and tragedy to wake them out of spiritual lethargy and bring them to a point of decision for Christ. Aleksandr Solzhenitsyn writes, "Bless you, prison, for having been in my life." The prison wasn't good. But God could bring good out of it.

The question each one of us must answer is, "Will I allow suffering to drive me to Christ for salvation and the power to be Christlike in character, or will I allow suffering to drive me into bitterness and despair?"

Seventh, the great news of the Bible is that God cares so deeply for hurting people that he has provided the solution for suffering and death. Jesus commands us to be agents of compassion and justice in a decaying world. To fight pain and suffering is not simply an option for a follower of Christ. It is an expression of his love for God. John writes, "This is how we know what love is: Jesus Christ laid down his life for us. And we ought to lay down our lives for our brothers. If anyone has material possessions and sees his brother in need but has no pity on him, how can the love of God be in him? Dear children, let us not love with words or tongue but with actions and in truth" (1 Jn 3:16-18). Followers of Christ use science, medicine, law, business, education and any other tool to alleviate suffering, prolong life, promote justice, and enhance the quality of life.

The great news of the Bible is that God is a suffering God. He suffered in Jesus Christ. God is not a philosophical notion floating in space. God is a personal being who became man in Jesus of Nazareth. He died on a cross to provide the ultimate solution for suffering and death. His solution is forgiveness and eternal life. Christ rose from the dead. Over a period of forty days he appeared to over five hundred people. He ascended to his Father in heaven. He promised to come again to destroy all evil, suffering and death. He will transform this chaotic, unjust world into an orderly, just world. "He will wipe every tear from their eyes. There will be no more death or mourning or crying or pain, for the old order of things has passed away" (Rev 21:4). If there is no all-knowing, all-powerful God who stands at the end of human history, justice shall never ultimately win. The wrongs will never be made right. Evil, suffering and death triumph.

But Christ taught that history was ultimately God's story.

The question is, "Have I accepted God's solution to the problem of suffering? Have I accepted Christ?" I cannot hide behind the question, "Why does God allow suffering?" But I can embrace God's solution for suffering by putting my trust in Jesus Christ for eternal life and allowing Christ to thrust me into a hurting world to administer his love, forgiveness and healing.

Question 12. Shouldn't God bear the responsibility for allowing evil to exist?

Some people object, "There cannot be a God of love because if there is a God who really loves, when he would look at the world his heart would break." In fact, the heart of God did break. When Jesus Christ was bleeding, dying on the cross, he cried out in his agony, "My God, my God, why have you forsaken me?" Jesus Christ, who had spent eternity with the Father, was separated from his father when he became sin on the cross. He took in his body the wrath of the holy God toward our rebellion.

Other people say, "God made the world. He is responsible. He should bear the pain and suffering." As we have already noted in the previous question, God did not create robots programmed to do good. Rather, he created persons, and to be a person means to have some freedom of decision. God created us and said, "O.K., now you have a choice.

You can either choose to do good or to do evil, to obey or to rebel." In both cases we chose the latter, and we are responsible for our choices.

But even though God is not responsible for evil, he loves us enough to voluntarily bear the responsibility for it. God was in Christ on the cross bearing all the pain and punishment we deserve for our wrongdoing. As Paul says in 2 Corinthians 5:21, "God made him who had no sin to be sin for us." And in the familiar words from Handel's *Messiah,* "All we like sheep have gone astray; we have turned everyone to his own way; and the LORD hath laid on him the iniquity of us all" (Is 53:6 KJV). Even though we sinned, our sins were put on Christ. How? Isaiah goes on to say, "He was oppressed and afflicted . . . ; he was led like a lamb to the slaughter" (53:7).

During World War 2 the guards at a Japanese prisoner-of-war camp would take the English soldiers out into the fields to do hard manual labor. At the end of one day the guards lined up the English prisoners and counted the tools. They found that one shovel was missing. A guard called out, "Who stole the shovel?" No one responded. The Japanese guard cocked his rifle and said, "All die! All die!"

Suddenly one Scottish soldier stepped forward and said, "I stole the shovel." Instantly he was shot dead. His comrades gathered up his body and the remaining tools and went back to the prisoner-of-war compound. Back in the prison camp, the Japanese guards counted the tools again. They found that no shovel was missing. The Scottish soldier had sacrificed his life so that his buddies might live.

Two thousand years ago God became man. His name was Jesus Christ. He lived a perfect life. He never did anything wrong. He did not deserve to die. He stepped forward and bled and died on a cross to pay the penalty that you and I deserve for having stolen, cheated, lied, dishonored our parents and ignored God. Your guilt and my guilt point to the wrong we have done. The cross of Jesus Christ points to the depth of God's love for us. You and I must decide to ask Christ for forgiveness and to commit our lives to him.

Question 13. Aren't the Bible's solutions to world problems outdated?

"What you're saying is nice," one fellow in New York said to me, but it is outdated. Jesus might have been fine for people living two thousand years ago in the Middle East. But now, men and women face problems of gigantic proportions. What does Jesus think the solutions are? Personally, I believe it's Marxism. I think the answer is political."

This is a very good point. It is one thing to talk about why evil exists. It is more important to ask, "What are we going to do about it?" There are a wide variety of solutions being offered for the problems facing humanity. Many people believe that more technology will solve our problems. But if we look at Nazi Germany, the most technologically advanced nation of its day, we see what it did with its knowledge. It perpetrated a global war and instigated genocide against an innocent people.

Others believe that education is the answer. If we just have more knowledge, certainly things will be all right. But

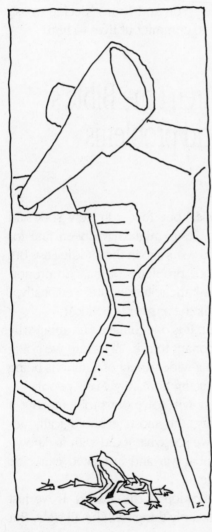

THE AMBASSADOR
PAUSES TO
RECONSIDER THE
APPROPRIATENESS
OF HIS OFFER
TO LEAD A
BIBLE STUDY
FOR THE
WARRING FACTIONS.

a bigger question needs to be asked. What are we going to do with our education and our technology? Are we going to use them to build more atomic missiles or find a cure for cancer?

Others think the answer is to be found in politics. But if that were the answer, wouldn't we already be moving toward a perfect political system? And where is the evidence that that is happening?

Still others say the solution is money. Pour enough dollars into a problem and it will be solved. But look at what the richest countries in the world face—high rates of depression, divorce, alcoholism, drug abuse and suicide. Instead of finding utopia, many have only found despair. Jesus pointed out time and time again that the problem with people is not technological, educational or political. It is a heart problem. We are twisted inside with our own self-centeredness. In Mark 7:21-23 Jesus said, "For from within, out of men's hearts, come evil thoughts, sexual immorality, theft, murder, adultery, greed, . . . all these evils come from inside and make a man 'unclean.' "

The problem with the world is not that we have the wrong political system. The problem with the world is you and me. Basically, we are selfish. We are motivated by what we can gain for ourselves. No wonder wars erupt all the time. No wonder the gap between rich and poor is so great. We are self-centered instead of God-centered. Jesus pinpointed the problem clearly: people are separated from God. We have chosen to go our own way.

When Jesus talked about the solution for our problems, he used some radical language. It may seem ordinary to us since we hear it so much. But when he first talked about being born again, about being born from above, he meant a dramatic change in one's life. He meant a brand new life. He claimed that if you and I would return to him and genuinely ask for forgiveness, we would be restored to a right relationship with God.

Jesus Christ was a realist, even though the way he's often presented today would leave you with some doubts about that. He realized that all the nice political and economic promises we make to each other will fade. He knew what it took to correct our problems—some radical surgery of the human heart.

Question 14. Why are Christians only interested in getting people saved?

Because I keep coming back to the basic necessity of having a right relationship with God, people sometimes think that is all I or other Christians are interested in. So let me be clear. It would be pointless for people to nod their heads in agreement with what I say, pray a little prayer and then go on in life unchanged. I don't preach, tally up the scalps of people who accept Christ and then walk away. If those I speak with do not go beyond acceptance to action, then I would be better off in another line of work.

To believe what Christ has done is to care for his people. To say, "Follow Christ's teaching," but neglect his creation is sin. It's like the Pharisees of Jesus' day who walked around in their religious garments and displayed their righteousness like clothes on a storefront mannequin but didn't lift a finger to help those in need.

Neglect is sin. James wrote, "What good is it . . . if a man claims to have faith, but has no deeds? Can such faith save him? Suppose a brother or sister is without clothes and daily food. If one of you says to them, 'Go, I wish you well; keep warm and well fed,' but does nothing about his physical needs, what good is it? In the same way, faith by itself, if it is not accompanied by action, is dead" (Jas 2:14-17).

Jesus Christ dynamites apathy as a sin against God and man. Jesus revealed that God created us for the purpose of loving him and loving each other. Jesus clearly defined love as giving, serving and laying one's life down for one's fellow man.

Mother Teresa, the great Roman Catholic nun who is helping the poor in Calcutta, India, to die with dignity, once said, "The biggest disease today is not leprosy or tuberculosis, but rather the feeling of being unwanted, uncared for, and deserted by everybody. The greatest evil is the lack of love and charity, the terrible indifference toward one's neighbor who lives at the roadside assaulted by exploitation, corruption, poverty and disease.

I am tired of hearing people call Christianity "pie in sky by and by." I am tired of hearing people say that Jesus Christ calls people to escape reality. The truth is that Jesus Christ commands his followers to get involved in this world as salt and as light. Salt preserves life. Salt gets into the food it is put on. Light dispels darkness. Light enables people to see clearly. Jesus Christ commands his followers to face reality, to try to understand people's pain and to struggle to change that pain into joy. Jesus Christ strips people of the opiate of materialism, hedonism and apathy. Jesus Christ wants to live in you to resensitize your conscience, to give you the moral power to stand for truth and to fill you with his compassion for a suffering humanity.

Suggested Reading

C. S. Lewis. *The Problem of Pain.* New York: Macmillan, 1978.

Jon Tal Murphree. *A Loving God and a Suffering World.* Downers Grove, Ill.: InterVarsity Press, 1981.

Michael Peterson. *Evil and the Christian God.* Grand Rapids, Mich.: Baker, 1982.

Philip Yancy. *Where Is God When It Hurts?* Grand Rapids, Mich.: Zondervan, 1977.

Four

How Can You Say Christianity Is Rational?

Instead of *worshiping God, many people worship their* skepticism. The apostle Thomas was once like this. Even though he followed Christ for three years, he wouldn't believe Jesus rose from the dead till he could put his fingers in the nail hole in his hands. But Thomas was an honest skeptic and worshiped Jesus when confronted with this graphic evidence.

God is not against skepticism. He is against dishonesty in our questioning. If our doubts about Christ are adequately answered, we have an obligation to follow him or else we cannot maintain our intellectual integrity. In the questions and answers in this chapter I seek to demonstrate just how certain we can be of Christ.

Question 15. Isn't believing in Jesus irrational?

Many people think that if they place their faith in Christ, they will have to commit intellectual suicide. They don't realize that Christ died to take away their sins, not their brains. Christians don't deposit their brains at the coat-check window and pick them back up on their way to heaven.

You can go to two extremes when it comes to the subjects of faith and reason. The first is to say that faith needs no reason: we just trust God without reservation then leap off the high board into the dark. But the fact is that Christianity does have a basis in history and in logic. There is evidence that Jesus was an actual historical person. The New Testament writings, the writings of Josephus and other first-century historians document this.

The second extreme is to say that if an idea is not logical, if it has no basis in rational thinking, then it has no place in my belief system. If you follow that thinking to its conclusion, then you have to throw out a lot of the miracles and healings in Scripture since logically people do not rise from the dead, logically the crust of leprosy does not fall off the body of its victim at the touch of a hand, and legs crippled for nearly forty years do not unhinge and become new because someone tells them to get up.

This is the balance people need to keep in mind when they say they are too rational to have faith, when they say they won't believe in something unless they can see it. Some have even said, "Cliffe, I wish I had your faith." Sometimes people mean this sincerely, but often they really mean, "Cliffe, I cannot be so stupid, so intellectually naive to believe all the superstition and garbage about God that you've apparently swallowed."

In a way that issue is moot. All of us believe in things we can't see. All of us place our trust in things that are not plainly evident. We believe in team spirit, patriotism, love, and goodness. Although we can't reach out and grasp any of these values, and though we so often see them misused and flaunted for selfish gain, we still believe they exist and often believe they have value.

Every one of us has faith. Every one of us believes in someone or something that gives us direction in life, that gives us security.

Peter Schaeffer wrote a play titled *Equus.* In the play a young boy begins to worship a picture of Jesus hanging over his bed. The boy's father, who is a devout atheist, rips the picture off the wall and replaces it with a photograph of a horse. The young boy, needing meaning and purpose, begins to worship the picture of the horse. The father gets more upset and sends the boy to a psychiatrist to have this fixation removed.

As the psychiatrist begins talking to the boy, he gains some understanding that was not apparent to the father. The boy does not have a fixation on Christ or a fixation on horses; the psychiatrist realizes that the picture gives the boy meaning, purpose and direction.

Schaeffer's point is clear. Whatever motivates us defines who we are. Live for pleasure—you are a hedonist. Live to amass wealth—you are a materialist. Live for personal happiness and fulfillment—you are a narcissist. Live to pursue knowledge—you are a rationalist. The British writer G. K. Chesterton said that when a person stops believing in God, he does not believe in nothing. He will believe in anything.

The question I put to those who tell me they won't believe unless it's rational is, "What is the object of your faith? Whom do you trust?" If the object of your faith is not trustworthy, it is not reliable. Real faith in something or someone that is trustworthy is not blind. Real faith will include the evidence to buttress it, and personal commitment. The faith of a Christian is based on the trustworthiness of Jesus Christ.

Jesus stated, "The Son of man did not come to be served, but to serve, and to give his life as a ransom for many" (Mt 20:28). Jesus gave us the evidence to back up his words; he consistently assumed the posture of a servant. Even at the very end of his public ministry, on the very night he was betrayed, he assumed the posture of the lowliest servant and washed his disciples' feet.

One day Peter asked Jesus, " 'Lord, how many times shall I forgive my brother when he sins against me? Up to seven times?' Jesus answered, 'I tell you, not seven times, but seventy-seven times' " (Mt 18:21-22). He spoke of complete and utter forgiveness.

Jesus gave us the evidence to back up his words. As he was bleeding and dying on the cross, his enemies taunted him. His response? He prayed, "Father, forgive them, for they know not what they do." He proved his trustworthiness; he proved his evidence was sound, and he asks us to trust him on the basis of that evidence.

A few people carry their inquiry even further. They say, "I must know *absolutely* that Christ alone is the truth before I can believe in him." This can be intellectual arrogance carried to an extreme. It requires that God give enough evidence of his existence to satisfy an insatiable intellect. This kind of arrogance demands that God meet every one of my requirements before I believe in him.

Suppose I demanded that my wife, Sharon, risk her life for me repeatedly to prove her love for me. Once would never be enough. The insatiability of my desire to know absolutely would be cruel manipulation, not intellectual integrity.

Yet many of us do exactly the same thing with God. We continually deny his past trustworthiness and say, "Now, what have you done for me lately?" This kind of wheeling and dealing is not intellectual prowess. It is cowardly manipulation. It also separates the proud from the humble. The proud say, "God, you meet these requirements, then *I'll* decide whether or not I want to believe in you." The humble person will look for evidence, discover it, and trust that if God was true to his word yesterday, he will be true to it today.

Confronting what I feel is intellectual dishonesty is never easy. It means having the discernment to know whether or not the intellectual arguments people offer are sincere. All of us need help in this area. If I confess my own intellectual and moral insincerity before God, I will be one step closer to being the kind of authentic witness God wants me to be.

Question 16. How can you prove God exists?

Often people challenge me, "Prove to me that God exists!" Perhaps they suspect that there is no way we can prove it. And they are right. But I ask, "Can you prove to me that your mother loves you or that just because she loves you today that she will still love you tomorrow? Prove to me that she won't poison your coffee tomorrow morning."

Can any of us *prove* that? I doubt it. We don't have final confirmation that our mother loves us, but we do have the evidence—she has cared for us in the past; she has accepted us; she has taken care of us when we couldn't take care of ourselves. The evidence is that she will not stop loving us tomorrow. The fact is that you and I can prove almost nothing. Instead we make our decisions based on evidence. So let me present some evidence (not proof) that God exists.

First, we live in a world that has unity, order and design. Order and design do not spring from chance. They come from an intelligent mind. Albert Einstein once said, "My religion consists of a humble admiration of the illimitable superior spirit who reveals himself in the slight details we are able to perceive with our frail and feeble minds. That deeply emotional conviction of the presence of a superior reasoning power, which is revealed in the incomprehensible universe, forms my idea of God."

A bit simpler and less profound statement of the evidence comes from Professor Edwin Carlston, biologist at Princeton University: "The probability of life originating from accident is comparable to the probability of the unabridged dictionary resulting from an explosion in a printing factory."

The Bible takes the evidence and makes it poetry: "The heavens declare the glory of God; the skies proclaim the work of his hands. Day after day they pour forth speech; night after night they display knowledge. There is no speech or language where their voice is not heard. Their voice goes out into all the earth, their words to the end of the world" (Ps 19:1-4).

Second, confronted by order outside ourselves, we crave order within. We crave purpose and meaning. Leo Tolstoy, the great Russian novelist, asked, "What is life for? To die? To kill myself at once? No, I am afraid. To wait for death till it comes? I fear that even more. Then I must live. But what for? In order to die? And I could not escape from that circle." Ernest Hemingway, the great American novelist, wrote, "Life is just a dirty trick, a short journey from nothingness to nothingness." Confronted by the meaninglessness of life, Hemingway decided to shorten the journey by committing suicide. If your birth was an accident and if your death will be an accident, then all that lies between is another accident we call life.

Adam Schaff, the Polish Marxist philosopher, writes, "From the point of view of the progress of nature death is entirely sensible. But from the point of view of a given individual death is senseless and places in doubt everything that he does. . . . Attempts to ridicule this do not help." Carl Jung, the famous psychologist, said, "The question of the meaning and worth of life never becomes more urgent or more agonizing than when we see the final breath leave a body which a moment before was living." Jean Paul Sartre, the French existentialist philosopher, wrote, "Man is absurd, but he must grimly act as if he were not." Why not? Why not face the logical ramifications of those assumptions? If there is no God, life is an accident. Humanity is absurd. Try and live out that view of reality. Most of us can't or refuse to. We insist upon attaching meaning and significance to our lives and actions. We have an innate drive to understand the purpose of our lives. Jesus said that we were created to love God with our heart, soul, mind and strength and to love our neighbor as ourselves. Our desire to live meaningful lives comes from the Creator who made us for a purpose.

Many of us pervert the purpose of life from loving God and loving people to the pursuit of superficial happiness and instant gratification. This makes sense for a few affluent, educated Westerners. It automatically condemns the majority of humanity to a meaningless existence. Jesus said, "For God so loved the world that he gave his one and only Son that whoever believes in him shall not perish but have eternal life" (Jn 3:16). Jesus Christ makes sense not simply for one sector of humanity but for the entire world. Jesus Christ brings meaning and purpose in life to the person in the Third World and to the person in the United States.

Third, where does human personality come from? I never see life come from nonlife. I never see being come from nonbeing. I never see personality come from matter and energy or from the impersonal. Dr. Jacob Bronowski, the American scientist, wanted to retain his unique personality. He wrote, "When I say that I want to be myself, I mean as the existentialist does that I want to be free to be myself. This implies that I too want to be rid of constraints (inner as well as outward constraints) in order to act in unexpected ways . . . I want to be allowed to be different from others. I want to follow my own way—but I want it to be a way, recognizably my own, and not a zig-zag. And I want people to recognize it: I want them to say, 'How characteristic!' "

Bronowski realized that modern science is reducing human beings to machines. "This is where the fulcrum of our fears lies: that man as a species and we as thinking men, will be shown to be no more than a machinery of atoms. We pay lip service to the vital life of the amoeba and the cheese mite; but what we are defending is the human claim to have a complex of will and thoughts and emotions—to have a mind. . . .

"The crisis of confidence . . . springs from each man's wish to be a mind and a person, in the face of the nagging fear that he is a mechanism. The central question I ask is this: Can man be both a machine and a self?"

When a chemical analysis of a human being is written up and handed in, the human being has not been completely defined. We each have a personality that goes beyond a simple listing of chemical ingredients in the brain. There is an "I" that at the end of a day can review the day's events and critique whether each action and attitude was worthwhile or not. Each of us has the ability to know himself. Behind human personality does not stand impersonal chance and fate but rather the personal Creator.

Fourth, the existence of values suggests that reality is bigger than simply cold matter and hot energy. The human appreciation of beauty and harmony suggests a Creator who created these values and the ability to recognize and appreciate them. Team spirit and patriotism, although not capable of being chemically analyzed or held in one's hand, are real values that many people enjoy. They point to a reality including more than simply that which can be scientifically verified.

Fifth, why do we trust our reason? If reason springs from

chance mutations and natural selection, why do we trust it to put us in touch with reality? What gives us the confidence that our reason is an accurate indicator of that which is true? Behind reason does not stand chance and fate but rather the rational Creator. He has created the universe and my mind in such a way that by observation and study I can begin to understand how the universe functions. Johann Kepler, the father of modern astronomy, peered out into the universe and exclaimed, "Oh God, I am thinking your thoughts after you!" If we do not believe there is a God, we must exercise blind faith in order to trust our reason which springs from chance. If we do believe in God, we trust our reason because we realize that both the universe and our minds were created by the rational Creator.

Sixth, we all have conscience, a built-in warning system that clicks in whenever we sense ourselves doing something we ought not to do. If there were no God, if everything were relative and situational, we wouldn't need this system; there would be no use for it. We also experience moral indignation over such things as child abuse, rape, apartheid, and the wanton destruction of human life. God has given us this indignation, this sensitized conscience, to enable us to differentiate between good and evil.

Now it is certainly possible for our consciences to become calloused, unfeeling from neglect or overexposure to evil. And it is difficult to live a life of consistency in a world that tries to go its own way without God. But the fact that we all begin with a conscience, is evidence of the existence of one who has imprinted an ability to sense good and evil into us.

Some argue that the human conscience is simply a result of conditioning by society, the consistent influence from the environment, and the pressure of the status quo. But a careful study of history refutes this. Almost every time a society has taken a step forward it was because an individual or a small group of individuals followed their conscience instead of popular opinion, the status quo.

Two white men in England, Newton and Wilberforce, fought for the abolition of slavery in the British Empire until they won in Parliament. Slavery was an important source of income for the British people. Great pressure was exerted on Newton and Wilberforce to quit their fight against slavery. But Newton and Wilberforce insisted on following their consciences instead of popular opinion.

Dr. Martin Luther King, Jr., was told by his society, "We don't want to hear from you. Don't you know your place?" But Dr. King insisted on following his conscience in his fight against racism in the United States. He refused to allow the status quo to set his moral agenda. Even when some of his partners in the struggle for equal rights tried to persuade him to use violence, he rejected their pragmatism and chose instead to follow the path of nonviolence his conscience recommended. His commitment to follow his conscience instead of the status quo led to a bullet being shot through his head. Today we honor him for following what was right instead of what was expedient.

Seventh, if there is no God, love is simply a chemical reaction, a biological drive, an animal instinct. In his novel *Nausea,* Jean Paul Sartre expresses disdain for young couples who try to escape the crushing absurdity of reality by retreating into the mythical realm of love. "I stop listening to them: they annoy me. They are going to sleep together. They know it. Each of them knows that the other knows it. But as they are young, chaste, and decent, as each wants to keep his self-respect and that of the other, and as love is a great poetic thing which mustn't be shocked, they go several times a week to dances and restaurants, to present the spectacle of their ritualistic, mechanical dances . . . "

If there is no God, only the natural is real. We are the result of chance mutations and natural selection. Reality is comprised of matter and energy evolved to different levels. Love is a chemical reaction. It is the sex drive or the drive to preserve the genetic pool as several Duke University students insisted. Reality does not include a real value of love. You cannot get the value of love from matter and energy. You simply have chemical reactions, one of which you like to get mystical about and call love. Sentiments are nice as long as they do not cause us to escape reality.

But my experience violently contradicts this world view. I have been the recipient of an unconditional love that was not motivated by either a sex drive or a drive to preserve the human species. I have observed people shower compassion and kindness on handicapped people and terminally-ill patients. Many human beings love others expecting nothing in return except continued racial slurs or slander.

Bishop Hasan Dehgani-Tafti prayed for the murderers of his son in Iran. "Oh God, we remember not only Bahram but also his murderers; not because they killed him in the prime of his youth and made our hearts bleed and our tears flow, . . . but because through their crime we now follow Thy footsteps more closely in the way of sacrifice. The terrible fire of this calamity burns up all selfishness and possessiveness in us; its flame reveals the depth of depravity and meanness and suspicion, the dimension of hatred and the measure of sinfulness in human nature. It makes obvious as never before our need to trust in God's love as shown in the cross of Jesus and His resurrection; Love which makes us free from hate towards our persecutors; Love which brings patience, forbearance, courage, loyalty, humility, generosity, greatness of heart; . . . Love which teaches us how to prepare ourselves to face our own day of death. O God, Bahram's blood has multiplied the fruit of the Spirit in the soil of our souls; So when his murderers stand before Thee on the day of judgment, remember the fruit of the Spirit by which they have enriched our lives, and forgive."

Jesus revealed that reality is bigger than matter and energy. Reality includes the supernatural God. This God is love. When God created us he put within us the innate ability to love. This love enables us to serve and sacrifice expecting nothing in return. This love comes from God and is available for each one of us.

Leighton Ford tells a story about the student riots at the Sorbonne, the French university, in the 1960s. A young man walked up to a bearded man who was rioting and asked, "Excuse me, sir. Why are you rioting?"

The bearded man responded, "I am protesting this lousy world."

The young man asked, "Do you believe in God?"

The bearded man replied, "No! I am an atheist."

The young man asked, "Do you love anyone?"

The bearded man lowered his head and said, "Yes, I love a woman by whom I have had a child. She is dying of leukemia."

The young man said, "Oh, that is too bad! Why don't you get another woman?"

The bearded man hauled back and almost hit the young man.

The young man quickly said, "Wait! You told me there is

no God. If there is no God, there is no such thing as real love. There are only biological drives. The woman dying of leukemia is losing her ability to satisfy your drives." Then the young man took out a Gospel of John which clearly states that there is a God of love. Behind the innate human ability to love does not stand the yawning void of chance and the impersonal. Behind every human's ability to love stands a loving Father who is in heaven. The bearded man walked away with something new to think about.

Eighth, even a cursory study of anthropology shows us that every culture has had some kind of belief system. Humankind is incurably religious. Blaise Pascal, the brilliant seventeenth-century French physicist wrote, "You and I have a God-shaped vacuum at the center of our being." Every culture shows evidence of the drive to fill this empty space with something satisfying religiously. You and I have a sex drive. There is a sexual relationship to satisfy that drive. You and I have an appetite for food. There is food to satisfy our appetite. You and I also have a drive to know God. The Bible reveals that God created us to know him.

Ninth, the historical evidence of Jesus Christ reveals that God does care and wants to know us personally. The evidence of his sinless life, the quality and clarity of his teachings, the love that flowed from him even during his painful death, and his historical resurrection from the dead point to Jesus being who he said he was—God in human form.

Nobody invented Jesus Christ.

Finally, consider that for two thousand years people around the world have claimed that this historical figure, Jesus Christ, has radically altered their lives. I'm not talking about a White-Anglo-Saxon phenomenon. I'm talking about people of different racial heritages and diverse economic and educational backgrounds all claiming that Jesus Christ has forever altered their lives and their thinking. I have seen blind women in Haiti tapping their canes to gospel music. I have heard some of the brilliant scientists and professors in the United States speak of their deep commitment and loyalty to Jesus.

The evidence is universal. The evidence is that God does exist. The evidence is that Jesus Christ is the truth.

Question 17. Why should I believe in Jesus?

Many people think the burden of proof rests on Christians to show why they should believe in Jesus. Whether or not this is true, I think there are reasons for believing.

The most fundamental reason for believing is because Christianity is true. Historically we can be as certain about what we read of Christ's life in the Bible as of any other recorded event. Psychologically we see how people's deepest needs are met by Christianity. Philosophically Christianity has enormous coherence as it shows what the ultimate meaning of life is.

But more important than Christianity being true is that Jesus Christ is the truth. He is God. He is the source and sustainer of all that is. He taught the truth. He lived the truth perfectly. He is the authority we can rely on. He is the ruler we should follow.

Another reason we should believe is because only Christianity can explain the dignity, honor and freedom of human existence. The Bible tell us that we are like all other animals in that God made us all. But we are also different. Human beings are created in the image of God and our purpose is to have fellowship with him. Can there be a higher, more enobling calling? If we live in a world without God, we are the children of a freak accident and the struggle for survival. We are pawns in the hands of fate and chance. If there is no God, ultimate meaning in life is impossible. We are given over to the unyielding despair of Bertrand Russell, the nihilism of Freidrich Nietzsche, the absurdity of Jean Paul Sartre. If there is no God, then there is no basis for the value, dignity and honor of human life. Christianity restores humanity to its rightful status by showing people that they are image-bearers of God.

Jesus' ministry frequently entailed restoring the dignity and honor of shattered human beings. One Sabbath Jesus was teaching in a synagogue. A woman was there who had been crippled for eighteen years. She was bent over and could not straighten up. She was a hunchback. When Jesus saw her, he called her forward and said, "Woman, you are set free from your infirmity." Then he put his hands on her and immediately she straightened up and praised God.

The synagogue ruler was indignant and said to the people, "There are six days for work. So come and be healed on those days, not on the Sabbath."

Jesus answered him, "You hypocrites! Doesn't each of you on the Sabbath untie his ox or donkey from the stall and lead it out to give it water? Then shouldn't this woman, a daughter of Abraham, whom Satan has bound for eighteen long years, be set free on the Sabbath day from what bound her?"

When he said this, all his opponents were humiliated. By going against man made religious traditions and seeking out the sick and the outcast, Jesus clearly demonstrates the dignity and honor of all of human life.

There is also an experiential component to why many people believe. We find that Jesus Christ loves us with a type of love that we have been searching for all life long. Christ loves us with an unconditional love. He loves us with the type of love that never fails and never quits. The love of Jesus Christ satisfies our deepest needs—needs that are inexplicable unless our Creator put them there.

Jesus approached the town of Sychar one day. Outside the town a lonely woman sat at a well. Jesus engaged her in conversation. After a while he told her, "Go, call your husband . . ."

She said, "I have no husband."

He said, "That's right. You've had five husbands and you're living with a sixth man."

"You must be a prophet," she said.

Jesus told the woman, "Everyone who drinks the water at this well will be thirsty again, but whoever drinks the water I give will never thirst. Indeed, the water I give you will become a spring of water inside of you that wells up to everlasting life. Woman, you have tried to fill your deep, human longing for love with sexual relationships. But you have failed time and time again. You are on your sixth try. I, as the living God, love you. I will fill that deep longing and desire, but not with sex. I will give you an unconditional love. Come to me" (Jn 4:1-26).

The question today is what or who are we using to meet that deep desire for unconditional love that we have? If we choose to meet that deep desire for love with any one or any thing other than Jesus Christ, we will ultimately be an empty, frustrated people. It is God alone in Jesus Christ who can fill that deep longing for a love that will not fail, for a love that will never say die.

Obviously these are not all the reasons for believing in Christ—one would need to read a whole library's worth of books to begin to cover all the reasons. The main issue for you and me is, what reasons do we have for *not* believing? Is it because we have honestly examined all the facts and found them wanting? Or is it that we fear God, that we are unwilling to change? We need to be careful and clear, because some day Someone who does not tolerate faulty logic will ask us to explain our reasons.

Question 18. Doesn't science disprove Christianity?

At the University of Maine in Orono a student went running through the crowd crying out, "Science disproves the existence of God. Science disproves the existence of God."

I asked, "What are you talking about?"

He said, "You know, evolution. Evolution is a proven fact. Evolution disproves the existence of God."

Evolution as an explanation of the origin of life is not a proven fact; it is a philosophy, a theory. But evolution as a description of a certain natural process in nature has much evidence supporting it. There are many Christian scientists and professors who believe in evolution as an accurate account of how some animals adapt to radiation, climate and topography. But they do not accept it as an explanation of how life began.

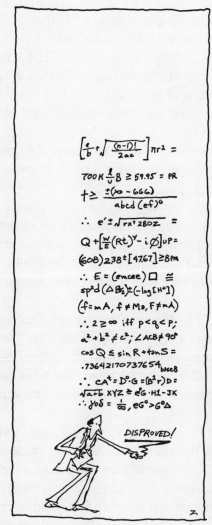

PROFESSOR
BUNSEN
REFUTES
2000 YEARS OF
CHRISTIANITY
IN ONE
50-MINUTE
CLASS PERIOD.

The book of Genesis seeks to answer two questions concerning the origin of the world. The first is, Who created? The answer is clear in the opening verse of the book, "In the beginning God" (Gen 1:1)—not "In the beginning hydrogen," not "In the beginning randomness." Rather, in the beginning God created the heavens and the earth.

The second question is, Why did God create? The Scriptures clearly reveal that God created human beings in his own image for the purpose of living in a deep love relationship with God and in deep love relationships with each other.

The book of Genesis does not seek to answer the question of *how* God created. I do not know how God created. No one does. It is entirely possible that God used the process of evolution to some extent to create life. Science is concerned about the observation and classification of facts. Science deals with natural processes. Genesis says nothing about these. I am grateful that the authors of the books in the Bible refrain from forcing into the text their scientific prejudice.

There is a story from *The London Observer* that illustrates the frailty of our understanding. A family of mice lived in a grand piano. They enjoyed listening to the music that came from the great player who they never saw, but who they believed in, because they enjoyed the music that came from the piano.

One day one of the little mice got especially brave. He climbed deep into the bowels of the piano. He made an astonishing discovery. The music did not come from a great player; rather, the music came from wires that reverberated back and forth. The little mouse returned to his family tremendously excited. He informed his family that there was no great player who made the piano music; rather, there were these little wires that reverberated back and forth. The family of mice abandoned their belief in a great piano player. Instead they had a totally mechanistic view.

One day another one of the little mice got especially brave. He climbed even further up into the bowels of the piano. To his amazement he found that indeed the music did not come from the reverberating wires, but rather from little hammers that struck the wires. It was those hammers that really made the music. He returned to his family with a new description of the source of the music. The family of mice rejoiced that they were so educated that they understood that there was no great piano player but that the music came from little hammers that struck the wires. The family of mice did not believe that there was a player playing the piano. Instead they believed that their mechanistic understanding of the universe explained all of reality. But the fact is that the player continued to play his music.

Modern science has done much to uncover the natural processes in the world. Daily we are learning more and more about how this world operates. But just because we understand how things work does not mean that there is not an intelligent mind behind the process. Albert Einstein expressed an awe and respect for the superior spirit or mind behind the universe. We should not make the mistake of getting so caught up with how things work that we ignore the Creator, the highly intelligent mind that is behind the intricate process.

Question 19. If Jesus is the truth, why do so many people reject him?

We usually assume that if something is true, most everybody will believe it. But that is simply not the case. And it is *not* the case with Christianity. Why? Because Christianity is not something we decide on like we decide on whether or not to believe in the existence of atoms. It is not a matter of sitting back, evaluating all the theories and then deciding which one best fits the facts.

Christianity is challenging. If it is true, our whole world will be turned upside-down. The main reason people reject Jesus is that he is threatening, more threatening than any army or group of terrorists could be. Jesus is threatening because he reveals things about God that shatter our worlds.

First, Jesus reveals that God is holy. Now I like to think I am a nice guy. I dress the right way. I speak the right way. I know how to do some of the right things. These things are important to me. I need them to have self-esteem and a good self-image. But then I am confronted by Jesus' life and teachings. He reveals that God is morally perfect and pure. Next to the source and standard of goodness, my veneer of goodness is stripped away. Jesus unmasks me, revealing that I am not the great guy I like to appear to be. Under the light of Christ I see my twisted motivations, my self-centeredness and hateful attitudes. Suddenly, I can no longer view myself as being good.

To avoid this threat I can deny Christ and thus ignore the holiness of God. It is that simple. By denying him I can continue to play the game of pretending to be a wonderful guy, a nice guy. I can continue to think that if there is a God, if there is a heaven, certainly I will make it, for I have done more good than wrong in my life. Certainly I am morally superior to the majority of people around me.

But because Jesus reveals how utterly holy God is, I am forced to realize that I am a rebel against God and that I do not really love all people the way I know I should. That is horribly threatening.

A second reason people reject Christianity is that Jesus reveals that God is all-knowing. Jesus said, "I tell you that men will have to give account on the day of judgment for every careless word they have spoken. For by your words you will be acquitted, and by your words you will be condemned" (Mt 12:36-37). The Bible also says, "Nothing in all creation is hidden from God's sight. Everything is uncovered and laid bare before the eyes of him to whom we must give account" (Heb 4:13).

That makes me very uncomfortable. There are certain parts of my life that I do not want anyone to know about. In fact, there are certain closets in my life that even I do not want to look into. They are private. It is impolite for others to look there.

But Jesus Christ confronts me with the fact that God sees every area of my life, that he knows me inside-out. He sees my good points and he sees my hypocrisy, my wrongdoing. If we stop there—and most people do—then these facts are tremendously intimidating. We want to escape. We want to deny that someone is at the keyhole looking in. We will pretend that no one can see the dirty closets in our lives. We want to be in control.

What most people do not see is that even though God sees all these things, he wants to cover us. Jesus Christ bled and died on the cross to pay the penalty for the wrong we have done. If we turn to him, he will forgive us and cover our moral nakedness. He doesn't want to destroy us because we are dirty; rather, he wants to clean us.

People also reject Christianity because Jesus reveals that God is just. He is the one who defines good and evil. If this God really exists, I am not free to do as I please. But if there is no God then as Dostoyevsky said, "All things are permissible." If God exists, then I cannot be wholly independent. Most people feel that freedom means we can do anything we please. But this is not the freedom Christ offers. He gives us the freedom to live the way God intended us to live. Adam felt this was not enough, and we agree. So to be independent we must either ignore God or deny him. We deny God so we might play God. We want to define good and evil for ourselves.

My brother, Stuart, went to Princeton University. He worked hard with fellow Christians to present the rational basis for faith in Christ. It became clear that too many Princeton students were rejecting Christ for moral reasons, not because of any intellectual problems. These students preferred to sleep around and cheat on exams. They knew that accepting the truth of Christ would require a change of lifestyle. If persistent dialog cleared the smokescreen, other objections would be vehemently raised to escape the call of Christ for commitment and a new life.

At State University of New York in Albany a student said, "The Bible is ancient mythology."

"Have you read it?" I asked.

"No."

"Read the book of Isaiah in tne Old Testament and the Gospel of Matthew in the New Testament. Then tell me if you still think the Bible is just ancient mythology."

I thought I would never see him again. But the next day he approached me and said, "I read Isaiah and Matthew. It is interesting literature. I think it speaks the truth."

"That's great! Are you ready to trust Christ for eternal life?"

He said, "No way. I have a very active sex life. I know Christ would want to change that. I don't want anyone to change that."

God is not sending anyone to hell. People are ordering God out of their lives. God will get out of their lives for eternity. That will be hell.

A fourth reason is that Jesus clearly revealed that God is all-powerful. If I think God is wrong or a threat to my self-sufficiency, how can I argue with him? How can I fight him? It is better to simply ignore him.

There are other reasons people reject Christ. Some people fear that Christ will not keep his promises, that he can't be trusted. We live in a world where relationships are mostly superficial. We live in a society where commitment and trust are dirty words. Suspicion, cynicism, skepticism are virtues. Don't trust anyone because people today are not trustworthy. After we have been burned by broken commitments and smashed promises, we find that we are unable to rely on anyone. Confronted by Jesus Christ we naturally are skeptical. The question "Will Christ keep his promises?" plagues us. But the evidence of his sinless life, perfect teachings, sacrificial death and historical resurrection proves that Jesus Christ is trustworthy. Jesus Christ can be trusted. He keeps his promises. He is saying to us, "Trust me and see if I let you down."

Another reason is that people fear that they will not be able to live for Christ. "I cannot live up to his high standard of morality. I cannot keep my promise. I fear being a hypocrite."

It's true. There is no way that you or I could live up to Christ's standard. But the good news is that Christianity is not merely following a set of rules tacked up on a wall. Real Christianity is a personal love relationship with the living Lord, Jesus Christ.

Jesus Christ comes to people who are disillusioned with religion but who are searching for spiritual reality. Jesus Christ does not call people into a self-help program. He does not command people to pull up their own bootstraps and simply try harder. Rather Jesus Christ calls us to humble ourselves before God, to trust Christ for forgiveness and for heaven, and to be willing to allow God to take up residence within us in the person of the Holy Spirit, to give us the moral power to become the people Christ wants us to be. We are not talking about religion. We are talking about relationship. Jesus said, "Here I am! I stand at the door and knock. If anyone hears my voice and opens the door, I will go in and eat with him, and he with me" (Rev 3:20). Jesus Christ wants to enter into a relationship with us. He waits for us to humbly respond to him.

Question 20. Can a Christian have doubts?

By this point you must be thinking, "Cliffe does seem sure of himself. I wonder if he ever has any doubts about Christianity." Of course I have doubts. Of course I have questions.

Every time I sin it shows that I really don't believe that what God says is true. If I did believe it, I wouldn't do what's wrong. The issue is not whether I doubt but how I am going to handle my doubts.

One day a grief-torn father came running up to Jesus and cried out, "Lord Jesus, your disciples have tried to heal my son but they failed. If it is possible, would you please heal my son?"

Jesus looked into the face of the father and said, "What do you mean, 'if it is possible?' All things are possible for the one who believes."

The father blurted out, "Lord Jesus, I believe, help my unbelief."

Jesus healed his son. The father was honest enough to admit that he had doubts. He did not commit intellectual suicide, but he was also humble enough to admit that his doubts hadn't gotten him anywhere (Mk 9:14-25).

Today we all have doubts. Are we going to be honest enough to admit that we do have doubts and are we going to be humble enough to admit that our doubts haven't gotten us anywhere in life? When I have doubts I tell Christ about them in prayer. I have found that whenever I am honest, sincere and genuine about my doubts and questions, Christ has gone with me through my doubts and given me a deeper understanding and faith. We can trust Christ with our doubts.

Prayer is not a cute formula. Prayer is a deep cry by a human being to the living God. God will meet us and satisfy us and fulfill us in unique and wonderful ways. No, we will never have all the answers. No, we will never be totally free from questions and doubts and sin. But Christians are people who have their eyes fixed intently on Jesus Christ, and they are pursuing Christ with everything in them. That is a lifelong pursuit. Christ invites us to make the lifelong journey of growing closer and closer to the living God. In the midst of our doubts and questions, we need to grab hold of Christ, and he will never let go.

The disciples told Thomas, "Jesus Christ is risen from the dead. We have seen him ourselves." But Thomas was a skeptic. Thomas was a doubter. Thomas said, "Not unless I can see Christ myself, not unless I can take my hands and put them into the nail marks in his hands, not unless I can take my hand and thrust it into the spear wound in his side, will I believe."

One night all the disciples were together. Suddenly Jesus stood among them. Jesus walked right up to Thomas, extended his hands toward Thomas and said, "Here Thomas, put your hands into the nail marks in my hands, put your hand into the spear wound in my side."

Thomas stopped doubting and believed. Thomas bowed down before Christ and said, "My Lord and my God." Thomas had questions. Thomas had doubts. But Jesus Christ met Thomas in the midst of those questions and doubts and Thomas believed.

Then Jesus told him, "Because you have seen me, you have believed; blessed are those who have not seen and yet have believed" (Jn 20:25-29).

The evidence of Christ's teaching, his character and behavior, his claims, his miracles, his death and his resurrection clearly point to him being trustworthy. Jesus is the truth. He is bigger than our doubts and questions. He is not jeopardized by them. He is only hurt by doubts when we use them to keep him at a distance. He wants to be intimate with us and will help us with anything that stands in the way.

Suggested Reading

Colin Chapman. *The Case for Christianity.* Grand Rapids, Mich.: Eerdmans, 1981.

Os Guinness. *In Two Minds.* Downers Grove, Ill.: InterVarsity Press, 1976.

C. S. Lewis. *Miracles.* New York: Macmillan, 1978.

Richard Purtill. *Reason to Believe.* Grand Rapids, Mich.: Eerdmans, 1974.

Del Ratzsch. *Philosophy of Science: The Natural Sciences in Christian Perspective.* Downers Grove, Ill.: InterVarsity Press, 1986.

Five

Why Are There So Many Hypocrites In the Church?

The world *expects a lot from Christians. And it should.* We have set very high standards for ourselves. We have high standards of love, of service, of community, of worship, of peace. It is no wonder then that when we miss those standards, it is quite obvious to a lot of people.

How do we reconcile our standards with our less than perfect behavior? How can we proclaim the validity of our message when so often our actions contradict it? These are important and often asked questions that deserve our attention in this chapter.

Question 21. Why are there so many hypocrites in the church?

A recent issue of *HIS Magazine* included a survey where they had asked college students, What is the first thing you think of when you hear the word *Christian?* The overwhelming response was "hypocrite." Wherever I go, this issue keeps coming up, "If Jesus is the truth, why are there so many hypocrites who call themselves Christians?"

We are all repulsed by hypocrisy. We all know that crusades, inquisitions and genocides in the name of Christ are huge perversions of what Christianity is supposed to be. One hundred fifty years ago there was a devout Jewish family in Germany. Their lives revolved around their Jewish community and customs. After the family moved to another part of Germany, the father returned home one evening and announced that the family would no longer attend the Jewish synagogue but would begin going to the Lutheran church. The young son was startled and asked for the reason for the change. His father responded that for business contacts and financial reasons it was more profitable to attend the Lutheran church.

The young man was angry and became bitter. He left Germany and went to England. He studied in the British Museum and wrote, "Religion is the opiate of the people." Today millions of people believe in his atheistic philosophy. His name was Karl Marx.

While we should reject hypocrisy, is it right to also reject Christianity? Aren't we being close-minded if we reject Christ because of a hypocrite? Isn't that like saying since I

REVEREND NICK
SIGNS ANOTHER
SELF-PORTRAIT,
PROVEN TO
REMOVE WARTS AND
UNSIGHTLY HAIR
FOR ONLY A
$29.95 DONATION.

once had a bad apple, all apples are bad? My landlady in inner-city Boston was beaten and robbed twelve times on the streets by young men of a particular skin color. My land-lady became a racist. She decided that all people with that color skin were thieves and thugs. That is close-minded prejudice.

To be open-minded and fair means to not prejudge peo-ple before we get to know them. To reject a person because of a stereotype is bigotry. Therefore, to be open-minded and fair when evaluating Christianity, we need to look to the first Christian, Jesus Christ, as he is portrayed in the eyewitness accounts in the New Testament. To judge Christ by someone who does not live up to what Christ taught or how he him-self lived is not only unfair, it does not make sense.

When we read the Gospels, we find that the sin Christ attacked most harshly was not adultery, lying or stealing, but hypocrisy. Hypocrisy is pretending to be someone you are not. Hypocrisy is lying about yourself. Hypocrites are blind to their need of Christ's forgiveness because they are hiding behind masks of moral superiority. Some people think they are Christians because they grew up in America or because they follow the Golden Rule, don't hurt other people and go to Easter sunrise service. Such cultural Christians refuse to face up to the cesspool of twisted motivations in each one of us. They think they are doing enough to get to heaven. This is hypocrisy.

Those who have come to Christ in faith know they are not morally or spiritually superior. They are all too aware of the evil within. This awareness motivates them to turn to Christ for forgiveness and help. As Aleksandr Solzhenitsyn, the great Russian novelist lay on a bed of straw in a prison camp in Siberia, he came to the understanding, "The line separating good and evil passes, not through states, nor between classes, nor between political parties either, but right through every human heart." When Solzhenitsyn saw that evil was not just a communist problem or capitalist problem but also his problem, he realized his need of a Savior. Solzhenitsyn came to Christ for forgiveness and life eternal.

The apostle Paul reviews his life and writes to the young Timothy, "Here is a trustworthy saying that deserves full acceptance: Christ Jesus came into the world to save sinners—of whom I am the worst. But for that very reason I was shown mercy so that in me, the worst of sinners, Christ Jesus might display his unlimited patience as an example for those who would believe on him and receive eternal life" (1 Tim 1:15-17). There is no hint of self-righteous arrogance. There is only praise for the God who saves wretched rebels and is patient with stubborn rascals. Hypocrisy, the parading of superficial morality, finds no lodging in the life of the individual who understands the horror of their evil and the depth of God's love in sending His only Son to forgive and save them.

Who were the hypocrites Jesus attacked? They were the pillars of the community, the ones held in high esteem by all, the ones known for their disciplined lifestyles and their knowledge of Scripture. They were the teachers of the law and the Pharisees: "Woe to you teachers of the law and Pharisees, you hypocrites! . . . You snakes! You brood of vipers! How will you escape being condemned to hell?" (Mt 23:33). Jesus was not soft on them at all! And why did he call them hypocrites? Because even though they knew their Bibles and even claimed to speak for God, they did not know God. In fact when God came to them in the person of Jesus Christ, they rejected him and even called him evil.

So why are so many Christians hypocrites? Because we are all sinners. Obviously people have twisted Jesus and used him to justify their own immorality, but Jesus himself condemns them. We all either try to hide our bad sides or we try to make them look good. Some even go so far as to cloak their sinful ways in Christian jargon and activities. But deep inside we all know that we fall short of living the way we know we should. No one can escape the charge of "hypocrite"—no one except Jesus himself. He is the only one who has lived up to God's standards; the only one who has perfectly lived what he preached. And it is only through trusting in the work of Christ that we can escape the penalty due our hypocrisy—separation from God and eternal death. By living within the security of Christ's love, we are freed to peel off masks and to become real, honest people.

Question 22. Why are there so many different denominations?

The lack of Christian unity is a problem that bothers Christians and non-Christians alike. If Jesus is the one great truth of the world, why do there seem to be so many versions of it in hundreds of denominations around the world? And if Jesus commanded his followers to love one another, why is there so much rivalry and even hatred expressed by Christian groups toward each other?

In John 17:23 Jesus prayed that the believers would be one so that the world might know that the Father sent him. He wanted his followers to be united. The fact that there are splits and divisions is sad. At no point did Christ want the Church to be fractured and fragmented. Jesus pointed out clearly that the problem with the world was that individuals have become self-centered. And Christians are no different. They are not perfect. Christians are forgiven sinners struggling to change, struggling with Christ's power to become more God-centered. But that is a lifelong process. Christians disagree and divide because they continue to struggle with self-centeredness. One Christian says, "I interpret this verse this way." Another Christian says, "I interpret the verse differently." They sometimes split over their disagreements. That is unfortunate. The church is Christ's hospital where hurting, fractured lives are being restored. The first requirement for membership in the church of Jesus Christ is to confess, "I am a sinner. I need help." I know of no other organization whose first requirement for membership is that you confess your faults.

At the same time, denominations do exist to express different styles of worship. It has been my privilege to worship in some churches where people are quiet and reserved. It has also been my privilege to worship in churches where the people have almost taken the roof off as they sing and praise the Lord. Both expressions of worship of Christ are legitimate. I would encourage you to find a church where you can worship Christ and learn about him with other believers. Find a church that views the Bible as the Word of God and not as a fertile field planted by human imagination. I am grateful that God is so great that he understands our unique, feeble attempts to love and adore Him.

Question 23. Isn't Christianity a crutch for weak people?

A woman at the University of California in Northridge challenged me: "Jesus is just a psychological crutch to help you deal with ignorance and fear. Because you are weak and scared, you have constructed a father figure in the sky to give you security. I don't need your crutch."

This attitude toward religion and Christianity in particular is very common in our modern world. It is assumed that if something meets too many of our needs, then it must be suspect; it is thought to most likely be a psychological defense mechanism. There are several responses to this line of reasoning.

The first is that I recognize that too many people have used Jesus Christ as a crutch. Jesus is sometimes used as a Rolaids tablet to settle an upset stomach caused by the fear of death. But Jesus Christ is not merely a sedative to give us peace and to ease our anxiety. Rather, Jesus Christ calls us to a radically new lifestyle.

Jesus challenges his followers to live lives committed to love, committed to justice. Becoming a Christian is not a supplement to our old lifestyles. Jesus calls his followers to have the courage to stand for truth and against lies and half-truths, to stand for the dignity and sanctity of human life and to fight the dehumanization we see happening around us.

At the same time, we should recognize that we all use some crutch to prop up our lives. It could be the prop of materialism, living to amass wealth. It could be the prop of hedonism, living to stimulate our nerve endings. It might be the prop of narcissism, living for ourselves. It might be the prop of careerism, living for personal achievement It might be the prop of personal happiness, living for self-fulfillment. Crutches help us to escape what we feel, to reduce the pain of emptiness at the core of our lives.

Jesus Christ comes and knocks those crutches away and challenges us to live for something bigger than ourselves. He challenges us to live to serve God and to serve a suffering humanity. To reject Christ and to buy into one of the crutches that our culture offers is to escape the challenge of life. Christianity doesn't allow us to hide behind crutches. Christ forces us to face life squarely and realistically.

Second, seeing Jesus Christ as a psychological crutch distorts the issue. The question of Jesus Christ is not a psychological question. It is a historical question. Jesus really lived, taught, died and rose from the dead two thousand years ago. It has very little to do with how well Jesus meets my needs. The evidence for Jesus is based on history. The historical evidence is that Jesus lived a perfect life and taught others to imitate his lifestyle; the evidence is that he bled and died on the cross; the historical evidence is that three days after he died he rose from the dead. Now the real question we must answer is, "Is this Jesus really the truth as he claimed to be?"

Third, while some claim that Jesus is a father figure in the sky that we project to meet our psychological needs, the psychological argument is circular. I could just as easily say that the reason people reject Jesus is because they have psychological hang-ups that prevent them from being able to trust a father figure. Just because God meets certain needs in us is no reason to reject him. In fact, it would be strange if he didn't fulfill certain needs we have. But again this is not the issue. We are confronted with the historical Jesus Christ who claims to be the infinite, eternal God penetrating human history two thousand years ago. Is he the truth or is he a liar?

The last thing I want to talk about is the true nature of sicknesses and cures. When I was on the basketball team in college, several of my teammates suffered knee injuries. Their legs were put in casts. They were given crutches to walk with. Since they were dependent on their crutches, does that mean I should have kicked the crutches from under them? As human beings we all have real needs. We have known guilt, loneliness and fear, and have experienced emptiness, sorrow and depression. Trying to escape them seems impossible. Regardless of how many sophisticated games we play to ignore it, we all face the finality of death.

To reject a cure because it is a cure seems silly. The exciting news is that Jesus Christ meets us in the midst of our very real needs. Jesus promises to forgive us and to wipe away the guilt that plagues us. Jesus Christ calls us into a relationship with the living God that will meet our deepest need for unconditional love. Jesus Christ knows our struggles, our fears and wants to replace them with peace and joy. We should only reject a cure if it is a false one, especially one that makes our condition even worse. But Jesus is the true cure to our real ailments. He only asks us that we try his medicine and see if it works.

You and I have real needs and hurts in life. It does no good to cover up these hurts and needs. That is escapism. Jesus Christ challenges us to face reality, and Jesus Christ promises to go with us through reality if we will invite him into our lives. The question today is, Are we willing to invite the living Lord Jesus Christ to go with us through life, through death and out the other side to eternity?

Suggested Reading
Michael Green. *Running from Reality*. Downers Grove, Ill.: InterVarsity Press, 1983.
C. S. Lewis. *Mere Christianity*. New York: Macmillan, 1981.

Six

Isn't the Bible
Full of
Myths?

The Bible is *the best seller of all time. More copies of it* exist in more languages than any other book in history. Unfortunately, it is also one of the least read.

So when I talk to others about what God says in the Bible, I get lots of questions. Isn't it full of myths? Doesn't it have lots of contradictions? Wasn't it written hundreds of years after the events it describes? Such questions can take a great deal of study to answer, especially if the questioner has specific problems or passages in mind. But there is some basic information people are unaware of that can satisfy the most common concerns. Here is a sampling.

Question 24. Isn't the New Testament full of errors?

Have you ever sat in a circle and whispered a secret in the ear of the person next to you? By the time the secret reached the end of the circle it was totally different. That is what some people claim has happened to the Bible over the past two thousand years. They wonder whether or not we can trust the Bible.

But the New Testament we have today is not something the church has created over the years. The New Testament we read today is based on over 5,200 early manuscripts or pieces of manuscripts all written in the original Greek. These Greek manuscripts were found throughout the known world of New Testament times from Rome to Alexandria. What is surprising is how little these manuscripts deviate from each other. Besides minor discrepancies that never alter the meaning of any text, the bulk of these manuscripts agree word for word with one another. There is no other ancient document that even approaches the New Testament in manuscript integrity and evidence.

In the past some scholars taught that the New Testament was written in the late second, third, fourth and fifth centuries after Christ. They then argued that the New Testament does not represent what really happened in the early church but is a record of the myths and stories that developed sometimes hundreds of years later. But one archaeological find smashed that whole school of thought. A fragment of the Gospel of John dated A.D. 130 was found in Egypt. Today this papyrus is in the John Rylands Library, Manchester, England. And no scholar thinks this is an original. They would say it was a copy of a manuscript written thirty to fifty years before that.

The New Testament was written in the first century. Luke begins his Gospel, "Since I myself have carefully investigated everything from the beginning, it seemed good also to me to write an orderly account for you, most excellent Theophilus, so that you may know the certainty of the things you have been taught" (Lk 1:3-4). Luke was a meticulous historian. John begins his first letter, "That which was from the beginning, which we have heard, which we have seen with our eyes, which we have looked at and our hands have touched—this we proclaim concerning the Word of life" (1:1). John claims to be writing an eyewitness account.

There are no contradictions in the Gospels which would cause us to question their credibility. There are some mysteries but no contradictions. Some used to claim that the pool in Jerusalem surrounded by five covered colonnades referred to in John 5 was a figment of John's imagination. Recently it was uncovered in an archaeological dig. Archaeology has validated many of the place names, governors, magistrates and emperors referred to in the historical narratives of the Bible. At no point does archaeology contradict the New Testament.

The apostolic fathers quoted the New Testament. A letter sent to the Corinthian church by Clement, bishop of Rome, about A.D. 96, quotes Matthew, Mark, Luke, Acts, Romans, 1 Corinthians, Ephesians, Titus, Hebrews and 1 Peter. Letters written by Ignatius, bishop of Antioch, as he traveled to his death as a martyr in Rome in A.D. 115, quote Matthew, John, Romans, 1 and 2 Corinthians, Galatians, Ephesians, Philippians, 1 and 2 Timothy, Hebrews, 1 Peter and 1 John. For these reasons—internal consistency, literary style of historical narrative, archeological evidence and a large collection of early Greek manuscripts—we can trust the New Testament as historically accurate.

We can read the New Testament for what it claims to be, an accurate, eyewitness account of the historical Jesus Christ. But now that we know the New Testament gives us an accurate picture of Jesus Christ and the early church, we must still ask, Is it true in what it says about God? This is a more complex issue that people have to decide for themselves. As a Christian I believe what Jesus and the biblical authors said is true and can be trusted. I believe that the Holy Spirit guided these writers to tell us what God wants us to know. Thus the Bible is more than just a history book. It is God revealing himself through the written word. It is the Word of God.

People who want to know if what the Bible says is true should try to read it openly and honestly. They should ask themselves, Do the Gospel accounts of the life of Jesus ring true? If someone were making all this up, would they do it this way? Do the characters in the Bible sound like mere religious fanatics who are out of touch with real life, or do the prophets and apostles sound like they have a handle on what is real?

Another interesting exercise is to compare Old Testament prophecies about the Jewish Messiah (for instance, Isaiah 52:13—53:12) with how they were fulfilled hundreds of years later in the life of Christ.

It is only as we explore the claims of the Bible, studying its teachings and putting them into practice to see if they work, that we will be able to know if the Bible is true and trustworthy. As we experience more of the truth contained in Scripture, the more we can trust it and the more we can put our trust in the one the Bible points to, Jesus Christ.

Question 25. How come there are so many interpretations of the Bible?

A woman in Knoxville asked me a question that I think is on the minds of many people: "Since there are so many different interpretations of the Bible, how can God possibly expect me to interpret the Bible correctly?"

Mark Twain once said, "It's not the parts of the Bible that I don't understand that disturb me, rather it's the parts of the Bible that I do understand that disturb me." The Bible is actually all too clear on the basics—God has revealed a few moral standards; we have broken those standards; the penalty for our breaking God's law is death and eternal separation from God and if we will turn to Jesus Christ and simply put our faith and trust in him, he promises to forgive us and to give us eternal life—these are all clearly revealed in Scripture. The Bible speaks plainly on the issues we need to understand. But Mark Twain put his finger on another problem: It is not that we are unable to understand; rather, the problem is that we often do not want to obey.

Besides the plain essential teachings, there are of course some parts of Scripture that are difficult to understand. But the promise of Jesus Christ is that his Holy Spirit will take up residence within each one of us and will begin to open our eyes to the truth that the Scriptures reveal. The apostle Paul writes in 1 Corinthians 2:14, "The man without the Spirit does not accept the things that come from the Spirit of God, for they are foolishness to him, and he cannot understand them, because they are spiritually discerned." I have a lot of friends who before they received Christ could not understand a thing in the Bible. But after they had come to put their faith and trust in Jesus Christ, the Holy Spirit opened their eyes so they could understand and apply God's Word to their lives.

Another reason Scripture is sometimes obscure is that it reflects places, histories, cultures and languages different from our own. The New Testament was written nearly two thousand years ago and the Old Testament was written four hundred to fifteen hundred years before that. Even though Bible translators have done a tremendous job in bridging the gap between biblical times and our own, there are still some things in the Bible we can't understand without knowing some background information. It is only as we learn the histories of Israel and the surrounding nations, the geography of the land and the way of life of the people will some passages in Scripture become understandable. But again I hasten to add that the essential teachings of Scripture are clear and obvious.

Question 26. Why do Christians always quote the Bible?

At the University of California in Santa Barbara an angry young man said, "Why do you always have to refer to the Bible? Why do you always quote the Bible and Jesus Christ? Can't you think for yourself?"

This is an excellent question. Why is the Bible my authority? First, consider an alternative. I could try and mesmerize as many people as possible and have them join my little group and follow me. But I don't think the real issue is, What does Cliffe think? Rather I think the real issue is, Has God spoken? Has God revealed truth? Is it possible to know God personally? If he has, then the best thing I can do is find out what he said and live by it. If God who lives outside and above time has entered time and space to give me information about my world that I could not otherwise know, then I should run (not walk) to my nearest Bible.

I have come to know God personally through Jesus Christ. I have experienced the trustworthiness of Jesus Christ. I know beyond a shadow of a doubt that he does not lie.

In Matthew 5:18 Jesus says, "I tell you the truth, until heaven and earth disappear, not the smallest letter, not the least stroke of a pen, will by any means disappear from the Law until everything is accomplished." Jesus is here referring to the Old Testament which he views as the Word of God and as entirely trustworthy. And the New Testament is the historical record of this Jesus of Nazareth and is also entirely trustworthy. (See Question #24 in this section.) That is why I quote Jesus and the Bible. We shouldn't just

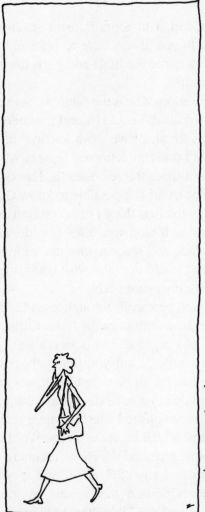

THELMA, ACCUSED
BY ROGER OF
NOT THINKING
FOR HERSELF,
HEADS HOME
TO CHECK HER
BIBLE AND SEE
IF HE'S RIGHT.

follow some flashy figure. Rather, we should focus on the historical Jesus Christ in the New Testament. We should listen to God speak throughout the Bible. As we put our faith and trust in Jesus Christ, then we will begin to know God.

Question 27. Isn't the resurrection a myth?

Can a thinking person believe in the historical resurrection of Christ from the dead? It is a nice story, people say, but who has ever seen a dead person rise from the dead. How can we believe it?"

While this question is limited to the resurrection, it actually challenges the possibility of all supernatural occurances. In a university setting this kind of skepticism toward miracles and the supernatural is common. It is assumed that only that which is observable and repeatable can be true.

What is ironic is that though science has gained us a tremendous amount of knowledge about our world, it can actually blind us from seeing who is behind the world— namely, God. When science goes beyond being a tool for the study of natural phenomena and becomes a philosophy of life, then we are in trouble. God cannot be observed and therefore cannot exist. No one living has observed a person rising from the dead; therefore, it could not have happened. But why are these assumptions made? Why can't a unique supernatural event occur? Because of scientific presuppositions. Ironically, these assumptions cannot be observed or proven. They can only be taken on faith.

There is nothing unreasonable about the resurrection. If we allow for the possibility of there being a supernatural realm, then unique divine acts can occur without contradicting reason (or science). The reason we have never seen a dead person brought back to life—especially one dead a couple of days—is because we were not there to see Jesus, the unique Son of God, the only one to lead a sinless life, being raised from the dead.

If we don't allow the possibility of a resurrection occurring, then the world is a neat and tidy place to live. But to be consistent, we must also reject the existence of thinking, emotions, beauty, ethics and so on—all the things that cannot be observed scientifically.

Since there is no reason for rejecting the *possibility* of a historical resurrection, we must turn to the Gospels, the eyewitness accounts, to find evidence for determining whether the resurrection is fact or fiction. As we read the Gospels we are struck by the vivid and realistic picture they paint of Christ's death and resurrection. The accounts record that Jesus experienced an agonizing inner struggle in the Garden of Gethsemane. He went through two sleepless nights. He was put through a Kangaroo court and beaten severely, convicted by a cowardly judge and flogged by mocking Roman soldiers. A crown of thorns was pressed into his skull. He was forced to drag his own cross to his execution. The soldiers drove nails through Christ's hands and feet, fixing him securely to the cross. For hours he hung there.

A soldier who had executed many by crucifixion looked into the face of Christ and said, "He is dead." But just to make sure, he jammed a spear into the side of Christ. We read that there was a "flow of blood and water" (Jn 19:34). Although they did not understand what the separation of blood and water meant in the first century, we know today that if you cut yourself and clotted blood flows out separate from watery serum, you have not been doing too much breathing in the last five minutes. It is a sign of massive heart failure and a clotting of the arteries. You are dead, stone dead.

They took the body of Christ off the cross, anointed it with about seventy-five pounds of burial ointments, wrapped it in strips of linen and laid it in a dark tomb. A great stone was rolled in front of the tomb and a Roman guard was assigned to make sure that no brave disciple would try to steal the body. The Roman soldiers understood they would be executed if the body was stolen. The soldiers were not playing games outside the tomb. They were guarding it.

Three days after Christ died he rose from the dead. The Gospels convey the shock and confusion one would expect from those who saw Jesus die. After some women had reported that the tomb was empty and angels had appeared to say Christ had risen, the disciples refused to believe it. After checking out the empty tomb for himself, Peter "went away, wondering to himself what had happened" (Lk 24:12).

Even after Jesus appeared to the disciples and ate with them and had them touch him to make sure he was not a spirit, there was still one disciple, Thomas, who was not there and would not believe. He said, "Unless I see the nail marks in his hands and put my finger where the nails were, and put my hand into his side, I will not believe it" (Jn 20:25).

One day all the disciples were together. Suddenly Jesus

stood among them. He walked right up to Thomas and said, "Put your finger here; see my hands. Reach out your hand and put it into my side. Stop doubting and believe" (Jn 20:27).

Thomas said to him, "My Lord and my God!" (Jn 20:28).

Paul writes in 1 Corinthians 15 that over a period of forty days Jesus appeared to more than five hundred people. Many of these eyewitnesses died for what they had seen—the dead Christ risen to life. They stood before Roman soldiers who said, "The decision is simple. Say, 'Caesar is lord' and live, or say, 'Jesus is Lord' and die!"

The early Christians said, "We have seen Jesus risen from the dead. Jesus is Lord!" They died, not for a belief, a religion, or a political persuasion, but for a person they had seen come back from the dead.

Too many people followed Jim Jones to their death in Guyana, mesmerized by a charismatic figure. Many have sacrificed their lives for a noble cause. But the early Christians died for a historical fact. They had seen Jesus risen from the grave. Paul states, "If Christ has not been raised, our preaching is useless and so is your faith" and "we are to be pitied more than all men" (1 Cor 15:14, 19).

If the early Christians had made up the resurrection story, they never would have died in such large numbers. Someone would have revealed the fabrication under penalty of death. You cannot get a large group of people to die for a known lie. History reveals that Peter, Andrew, Philip, Simon the Zealot, James the son of Alphaeus, and Bartholomew were crucified. Matthew and James the brother of John were put to death by the sword. Thaddaeus was shot through with arrows. James the brother of Jesus was stoned. Paul was beheaded. Why? Because they had seen Jesus risen from the dead. They were willing to die for what they had seen.

Scientifically we cannot prove that Jesus Christ was resurrected from the dead. But, as we have seen, proper science does not exclude this possibility. We must depend on the historical reports of those who saw everything first hand. Whatever happened, we know that the event changed the lives of these individuals. They went from being fearful and confused to being wise, loving, brave and even willing to die for what they had witnessed. So the issue boils down to, Is it reasonable to believe these men?

Question 28. When will Jesus return?

I am often asked, "When will Jesus Christ return?" My answer is one of the few I am absolutely certain about, "I do not know." In fact, we are to watch out for people who say they do know. Jesus clearly said, "No one knows about that day or hour, not even the angels in heaven, nor the Son, but only the Father. As it was in the days of Noah, so it will be at the coming of the Son of Man. For in the days before the flood, people were eating and drinking, marrying and giving in marriage, up to the day Noah entered the ark; and they knew nothing about what would happen until the flood came and took them all away. That is how it will be at the coming of the Son of Man. Two men will be in the field; one will be taken and the other left. Two women will be grinding with a hand mill; one will be taken and the other left. Therefore keep watch, because you do not know on what day your Lord will come" (Mt 24:36-42).

Jesus promised that he would return but he clearly warned against trying to set a date. He did promise that he would close out history when he returned in power and great glory.

I do not know when Christ will return, but I do know that he will return. He promised to come again. He clearly taught that there would be a day of judgment and then a separation. Some will spend eternity with Christ in heaven; others will spend eternity separate from Christ in hell. The issue will be, How did you respond to the love of Jesus Christ? How did you respond to his truth? We are not to live for a world that will decay and be destroyed. Rather, we are to live for the eternal God, the Lord Jesus Christ. If we transfer our allegiance from that which will rust, decay and be destroyed to the eternal God, we will have eternal life, which is available to all who trust in his Son, the Lord Jesus Christ.

Suggested Reading
Norman Anderson. *Jesus Christ: The Witness of History.* Downers Grove, Ill.: InterVarsity Press, 1985.
F. F. Bruce. *The New Testament Documents: Are They Reliable?* 6th ed. Downers Grove, Ill.: InterVarsity Press, 1981.
John R. W. Stott. *The Authentic Jesus.* Downers Grove, Ill.: InterVarsity Press, 1986.
——————— . *God's Book for God's People.* Downers Grove, Ill.: InterVarsity Press, 1982.

Seven

What's Wrong With Having a Good Time?

Every single day *we make moral decisions that flow* from our view of reality. Will we cheat on this expense report? Will we crack a racial or an ethnic joke? Will we have sexual relations with anyone we feel attracted to? Will we lie to get ahead or to get out of a jam or to avoid something unpleasant about ourselves?

We hate it when people lie to us or try to deceive us. Yet for some reason we aren't quite as upset when we find ourselves behaving the same way toward others. Some students have told me how appalled they were that someone would try to steal their boyfriend or girlfriend from them. But then they have to admit that from time to time they've also cast a wandering eye toward someone else's boyfriend, girlfriend, or spouse. We find it appalling that the United States once sanctioned slavery and that apartheid (legal separation of the races) is the law of the land in South Africa. Yet how often have we laughed at the expense of someone of another background when we heard the punch line of a racist joke or told one ourselves?

If we are really honest with ourselves, we realize that our own good intentions often falter. We begin to understand that it is not in our nature to be sweet, gentle and pure all the time.

Many people I've spoken with tell me that morality is relative, that it depends on the situation you're in. Yet in the same conversations the same people will confess that they are plagued by guilt. In spite of their intellectual assent to situational ethics, they still go through periods of great fear and doubt about their actions. When they boil it all down, guilt is draining all the joy and spontaneity from their lives.

Some of these people want to accept Christ, but they want it on their terms. They don't want Christ to dwell in them; they'd rather just use him as an additive to get them out of a jam. They think he is Jesus, the quick fix. But Jesus refuses to be manipulated by us in this way. He comes as a radical alternative to the old way we've chosen to live.

It is difficult to convince people that Jesus doesn't want to change our lives because he wants to cut all joy out of our lives. Rather it is because he knows how we operate best. He knows that we function the way we're meant to when we're restored to a proper relationship with our Creator and his creation. He knows that this will give us the most satisfaction and joy possible in life.

The guilt many feel will drive them in one of two directions. The first is to try to get rid of it by plunging even further into their old lifestyle until they can rationalize it completely or until it destroys them.

The second option is for people to reject their own feelings of moral superiority and turn to the mercy and forgiveness of Jesus Christ. Their guilt can drive them to realize their personal need and to understand that Christ did not come to condemn and reject, but to accept and restore.

We face many moral and spiritual battles in the world. Satan seeks to capture our allegiance through a myriad of venues—materialism, hedonism, narcissism, power and sex. I have talked about a lot of these issues to many people. Here are the questions they ask most frequently.

Question 29. What's wrong with sex?

Once a young lady shouted out from a crowd of students, "What's wrong with sex? Is God against sex? Sex is fun. Is God against fun?" A group of fraternity guys roared their approval.

My response was to ask who invented sex. Was it thought up by some of our media heroes? No. God invented sex. It's one of his most beautiful gifts to us. He is not a celestial grinch grumbling at anyone in the universe who might be having fun.

God could have arranged for procreation to take place when a man and a woman mixed their earwax at the end of a Q-Tip. But he didn't. Instead he gave us the gift of our sexuality. As with every gift, however, we have a choice. We can follow the directions and use the gift as it was intended, or we can throw the instructions away and try to put it together the way we want it. Like lots of gifts God has given us, we've twisted sex for our own selfish and sometimes abusive purposes. And if we share that gift with just anyone, we stand a great chance of having it damaged. Sexuality is not a meaningless addition to life designed to give us a few cheap thrills. God gave us our sexuality for several important reasons.

First, God gave it to help take away our aloneness. Genesis 2:18 reads, "The LORD God said, 'It is not good for the man to be alone. I will make a helper suitable for him.' " Woman to man. Man to woman. Each a gift to the other. God did not desire loneliness to be an ongoing part of our existence. He wanted men and women to live together in a relationship of deep commitment—sexually, emotionally and spiritually. This deep commitment, when worked on daily, will result in a level of acceptance that will never quit. There will be the freedom of knowing that there is someone who accepts you exactly as you are, with all your character and physical defects.

Second, God created sex as the means of procreation. This is intimately intertwined with what God intends for families. We are all very familiar with the great emotional and psychological damage that has been done to children in recent decades with the high rate of divorce in society. God's design is for children to grow up in the secure environment of parents who are life partners. That can't happen when we play fast and loose with sex.

Third, God gave us sex to help create a permanent bond of trust in a marriage. Why do we hurt so much when our husband or wife is sexually unfaithful? Because when we give ourselves to our spouse sexually, we are saying, "I am willing to give myself to you completely, to become one with you physically as well as spiritually and emotionally." We are making ourselves completely vulnerable and completely open to some deep emotions. We are entrusting ourselves completely to someone else.

That trust is violated at a great cost—in damaged egos, damaged pride and broken trust. There can be forgiveness and there can be reconciliation, but the healing process can take a long time. That is why God designed our sexuality to be shared with one other person in the context of marriage. He knows what an incredibly fragile part of our being it is and what can happen when it is handed out and passed around to any interested party. It can leave behind a trail of broken and fragmented people.

Another reason God intended sex to be exclusive is guilt. All of us have a conscience that serves as an alarm system. An alarm system is supposed to give a warning to an owner that the property is in jeopardy. But if the owner kept tripping the alarm, he or she might burn out the system. Then when a danger really threatened, the system would be useless. Likewise we can sear and damage our consciences so badly that they will quit warning us when we are about to do something wrong.

A lot of people have told me, "Cliffe, I'm having sexual relations with several different people at this stage of my life, and I don't see anything wrong with it. When the time comes to get married and settle down, I will."

My response to this attitude is to ask, "What makes you think that walking down a church aisle is going to stop you from sleeping around? If the woman you marry has slept around before she married you, what makes you think she won't go back to her old pattern of behavior—especially if your relationship ever became a bit strained? And what makes you think that you won't do the same?

"Premarital sex can sow great seeds of distrust in a marriage. If you are used to a variety of sexual partners, what makes you think you are suddenly going to be satisfied with just one? Our sexuality is a very strong but very fragile and vulnerable part of who we are."

Extensive premarital sexual activity can lead us to trivialize the sex within marriage. But God intended sex to be a deeply fulfilling part of an exclusive marriage relationship. To treat it otherwise is to deprive ourselves of the enjoyment of all that sex can be.

Question 30. What's wrong with sex if you're in love?

I'll never forget the conversation I had with Todd in Florida. He said, "Cliffe, I really love my girlfriend. She really loves me. And we have sex together. There can't be anything wrong with it since we really love each other. And it feels so good. Why is God against our having sex just because we're not married?"

"I think it's great that you love your girlfriend so much," I said. "Tell me about your love for her." For the next couple of minutes Todd romantically described how much she meant to him. Then I asked, "If she was in a car accident and her face was scarred badly for life, would you still love her? Would you still be committed to her?"

I respect this man for his honesty because he replied, "No way. If her face was messed up, I would drop her and go find someone else better looking."

"That's very interesting," I said. "Well, could you tell me about the way she loves you." And for another couple of minutes Todd expressed the deep love and commitment she had for him. When he finished I asked, "Now tell me, if you were in an accident and your face was rearranged, would she still love you?"

"Yes," he said. "I believe that she loves me so deeply that even then she would be committed to me."

"Well that's great, Todd. It's quite clear that she is ready to marry you, to commit her life to you till death parts you. But it doesn't seem like you are ready for such a commitment. You seem to be using her for a thrill. And if she loses her ability to turn you on, if someone else comes along who can give you a bigger thrill, then you are going to walk out on her as quick as you can. That is not love. That is lust. That is using someone as a sex object, a trinket for your pleasure. You are dehumanizing her by treating her like a thing, like a thrill-making machine. Christ says we are to treat people with respect and dignity. And in the arena of human sexuality, that means a lifelong commitment to one person.

"It's not too late to change. If you put your trust in Christ, he can forgive you and give you the power to stop dehumanizing others. That is what I wish for you, Todd. I wish for you honesty, dignity, integrity and love that will last. And all these can come to you in Christ."

Question 31. What's wrong with homosexuality?

Several people have asked me about homosexuality as well as heterosexual freedom. My first response is to apologize to homosexuals for the way they have been treated as dirt and scum by some "Christians." Homosexuals are not inferior humans. According to the Bible all human beings are created in the image of God. This image has been defaced horribly in each one of us. But each of us has equal value and dignity given us by our Creator.

Second, life is not an accident. It is a gift given each of us by God for the purpose of loving God and all people. In the same way that life is not an accident, so our sexuality is not an accident. No playboy or playgirl invented sex. God thought up sex. He gave us sex to communicate the deepest love, trust and companionship possible between one man and one woman. I, through my heterosexual lust, have perverted the gift of human sexuality just as my homosexual friend has through his or her homosexual lust. We both stand guilty before God. The great news of the New Testament is that God offers us both forgiveness through Jesus Christ.

Jesus was teaching in the Temple one day. A group of men came running to him pushing a woman in front of them. They made her stand before Jesus and said, "We caught her in the act of adultery. In the Law it says we are to stone such a woman. What do you say we should do?" Jesus bent down and wrote in the dirt. The men pressured him for an answer.

Jesus answered, "If any of you is without sin, let him be the first to throw a stone at her." In other words, "If any of you men have never lusted, go ahead and stone her." Then Jesus bent back down and wrote on the ground. The stones slipped out of their hands. They left one at a time.

Jesus stood up, looked the woman in the face, and said, "Woman, where are your accusers? Have none of them condemned you?"

She said, "No one, sir."

Jesus declared, "Neither do I condemn you. Go now and leave your life of sin." The woman came to Christ guilty, expecting death. Christ was not there to condemn but rather to forgive. Jesus was saying, "Woman, I will drag a cross up a hill, be nailed to it, bleed and die on it, in order to pay the just penalty for your sexual immorality. I forgive you because you acknowledge your need and my authority. Now I free you to live a new life, a sexually pure life."

At Northwestern University a basketball player laughed and said, "You've got to be kidding. You are asking me not to want to have sex with the many good-looking women I see every day. What do you think I am? A wimp?" It was clear I was attacking his view of manhood.

Another student said, "I was born homosexual. How can you possibly expect me to change who I am and how I behave?" It was clear I was threatening a key part of his identity.

A follower of Jesus Christ is not a person who simply tries to live up to a moral code. Real Christians are those who have invited the Lord Jesus Christ to take up residence within them. Christ's resurrection power is at work in their lives, transforming their identities and behavior into that which is pleasing to Christ.

It is possible that you were born with an inclination to lie, tell racist jokes, steal, set fire to buildings, have sex with several people or have a homosexual relationship with one partner. Jesus proclaims his desire to live in us to work with us to restore the defaced image of God.

Jesus defines manhood for the Northwestern University basketball player as the strength and integrity to wait till he has made a lifelong commitment to one woman before he enjoys having sex. Any dog can have sex with many different dogs. It takes a man to be committed to one woman and to experience fulfillment in that companionship.

Jesus defines sexual identity for the Northwestern University homosexual as freedom from the twistedness of homosexuality and freedom to either celibacy or a heterosexual relationship with a spouse. The power to change comes from the risen Christ. The apostle Paul writes, "I pray also that the eyes of your heart may be enlightened in order that you may know the hope to which he has called you, . . . and his incomparably great power for us who believe. That power is like the working of his mighty strength, which he exerted in Christ when he raised him from the dead and seated him at his right hand in the heavenly realms" (Eph 1:18-20). I have experienced this power in my life. It is available to you if you will trust in Christ.

Question 32. What's wrong with getting drunk?

Another line of questioning in the area of personal morality that comes up often are the subjects of drugs and alcohol. At Wake Forest University I was invited to speak to the football team. One of the players raised his hand and asked simply, "What's wrong with getting drunk? What's wrong with unwinding a bit?"

Many people get drunk to escape the reality of their lives. They don't want to handle life on its own terms because it is too difficult to face. They want to block out the fearful emotions that may surface. And you know what? Alcohol works for a time—maybe a few weeks, maybe a few months, maybe for years. Alcohol does block out and submerge the part of ourselves we don't want to face.

But one day the rent comes due. Alcohol doesn't do its job anymore. At that point the heavy drinkers can go in one of two directions. They can face up to their situation and get some help or else deduce that their problem is that they are not drinking enough.

Jesus Christ is a realist. He does not counsel us to run and hide when we face the severe problems that life often hands us. He says, "Come to me, all of you who are weary and burdened and I will give you rest. Take my yoke upon you and learn from me. For I am gentle and humble in heart, and you will find rest for your souls. For my yoke is easy and my burden is light."

What Jesus is saying is simply, "I am strong and gentle enough to shoulder whatever you face. Put your trust in my strength, not in an artificial prop."

Another reason people get drunk or get high is to shortcut the hard work of human relationships. Whenever we become vulnerable before people, there is always a risk that our honesty will be ripped apart and taken advantage of. A few sips of this, a few hits of that, and all of a sudden we

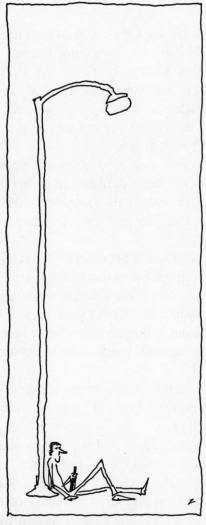

MERLE
KNOWS THAT
THERE'S
SOMETHING
WRONG WITH
GETTING DRUNK,
BUT HE CAN'T
REMEMBER
WHAT IT IS.

have an aura of protection. We're witty and urbane conversationalists. We may not remember what we said in a few hours, but we were sure clever while we were saying it.

But Jesus asks us to go to him for security and not to a chemical. The true strength found in a relationship with Christ is stronger than any drug-induced mask we may attempt to put on, because he helps us face life more fully.

Finally, the most priceless gift God has given us is our body, his dwelling place. When we choose to artificially alter our behavior, induce courage or speed up or slow down our reaction time, we're destroying that gift. We may be strong enough now to escape the physical consequences of drug or alcohol addiction, but a day will come when the damage we've done to our sytem will be irreversible.

When Christians share the good news of Christ they have the obligation to offer a genuine hand of friendship and care. It is their obligation to show people that there is security in a relationship with Jesus Christ among a fellowship of like-minded friends. All of us are under constant pressure to compromise our values and our behavior. Many people get drunk just because "everybody else" (that is, some of their friends) are doing it. Social pressure pushed them to do something they might have otherwise chosen not to do. Unless Christians can show with their words and with their lives that Christ offers secure friendships, people will almost certainly go somewhere else to find it.

Question 33. What is sin?

Questions of personal morality are very popular when I

speak. But sin is a lot more than just fooling around sexually or getting drunk or stealing. In fact, sin is also a lot more than social injustice. Certainly we abhor racism, greed, institutional corruption, poverty and world hunger. But all of these are only a small portion of the sin problem.

We can say a number of things about what sin really is. First, *sin is breaking God's law.* It's not a minor mistake, a little miscalculation or a slight error in judgment. It's violating God's standards which are summarized in the Ten Commandments. We've all heard that we are not supposed to steal or lie or murder or commit adultery. Now some of us might claim to do pretty well with that list. "I've never killed anyone or even shoplifted," we might say. But in the Sermon on the Mount, Jesus defines sin as more than an action. He says it is also an attitude.

> You have heard that it was said to the people long ago, "Do not murder, and anyone who murders will be subject to judgment." But I tell you that anyone who is angry with his brother will be subject to judgment. . . . You have heard that it was said, "Do not commit adultery." But I tell you that anyone who looks at a woman lustfully has already committed adultery with her in his heart. . . . You have heard that it was said, "Love your neighbor and hate your enemy." But I tell you: Love your enemies and pray for those who persecute you, that you may be sons of your Father in heaven. (Mt 5:21, 27-28, 43-45)

These statements are simple and the implications are clear. Sin is not just a wrong action. It is a wrong attitude. Jesus says, "Murder is wrong, but so is hatred. Adultery is wrong, but so is lust. Not only is striking back wrong, so is holding a grudge against someone who has hurt you."

Christ's teachings are in utter contradiction to the way our culture asks us to look at life and tells us to behave. Adulterous relationships are portrayed as a stage of life that most of us will go through at one time or another. We are encouraged to treat our enemies or those who disagree with us not with a spirit of reconciliation, but with a spirit of hatred and an eye toward revenge. After all, we're not going to let anyone walk over us!

But most of the problems I see today revolve around the intense competition for success in a career. Many in their quest to get ahead begin to resort to the models the culture offers. Drive and ambition will get them to the top—at least that's the image they're presented with. The images they do not see are strewn with broken relationships and the broken people who have been walked over on the way to someone else's advancement.

Second, *sin is rebellion against God.* It is taking the gifts God has given us and perverting them. People have taken the creative and restorative powers God has given them to destroy life rather than save it. We have taken the intellect God has given us and used it to build tools of destruction.

I am amazed, especially in my own life, at the subtle, and not so subtle, ways I have taken what God has given me and used it for other than what he intended. Too often I have taken the ability God has given me to speak and torn people down rather than build them up. All too often I have taken the sight and insight God has given me and focused them on violence, lust and evil, instead of using these gifts to focus on what is pure and pleasing in God's sight. All too often I have seen people hurting and ignored them. That is a perversion of the faculties God has given me.

Even one sin makes us a rebel. That's why breaking one of God's laws is the same as breaking all of them. "For whoever keeps the whole law and yet stumbles at just one point is guilty of breaking all of it. For he who said, 'Do not commit adultery,' also said, 'Do not murder.' If you do not commit adultery but do commit murder, you have become a lawbreaker" (Jas 2:10-11). This is not arbitrary on God's part. It just means that we can't claim that our sins are "not as bad" as someone elses'. Any claim to spiritual pride falls flat in the face of our insurrection against God.

In fact, the real heart of sin is false pride, the arrogance of the human heart that says, "I am at the center of the world. I am my own god, and I make up my own rules. What I am doing in this life should be paid attention to because it is of paramount importance." Our false pride tells us that we have the attributes of God—we are all-knowing and all-powerful. We think we know how best to run things, how to treat others, and what to do and what not to do.

Pride—the need to control—is at the heart of all sin.

Third, *sin is lostness.* Probably the best portrayal of this aspect of sin found in Scripture is in Jesus' story about a father who had two sons. One afternoon his younger son came to him and said, "Dad, I've had enough of things around here. It's boring. There's too much work to do, and all your regulations are holding me back. Right now what I want is the money that I would receive upon your death."

The son took the money and ran. He traveled far away from the safety and shelter of his father's house to search for the zest he thought could be found somewhere else. He felt it was time for him to make his own rules. This young man was like many of the students I speak with as I travel across the country. They are tasting for the first time the thrill of independence when their parents are far away, and they have no one making rules for them.

A good portion of the students I encounter begin to grab for the brass ring their culture and their peers tell them will bring them happiness—the props of sex, materialism, self-ishness, drunkenness, false friendship and easy money. These props may not fail for quite a while, but they will fail eventually. When they do, the fall is hard and long.

The story was the same with the prodigal son. One day his money ran out and a famine hit the country. The young man got hungry and cried out for help, but everywhere the answer was the same—no cash, no food. One man finally said he would help. "Sure, son," he said. "Why don't you go feed my pigs? You can eat what they don't."

The offer was insulting because the young man was Jewish, and to the Jews the meat of the pig was unclean. A Jew with a job feeding swine was about as far down the social scale as you could go. But isn't it true that we often have to slip that far down before we can hear the voice of God calling us back and realize just how far we've strayed?

Jesus describes the young man's turnaround in a poignant phrase. Amidst the pigs and the mud and the rotting husks of food, Jesus says, "The young man came to his senses." He remembered his father's love—and he knew that the servants in his father's home were being treated better than he was.

In the middle of that pigpen, the young man swallowed his last ounce of pride and resolved, "I will set out and go back to my father and say to him: "Father, I have sinned against heaven and against you. I am no longer worthy to be called your son; Make me like one of your hired men' " (Lk 15:18-19).

I can imagine the son rehearsing this speech over and over again as he headed back toward his father's home. But he didn't need to. When the father caught sight of his son, the father ran toward him and embraced him. The son gave his rehearsed speech, but the father was having none of it. "Quick! he said. "Bring the fattened calf and kill it. Let's have a feast and celebrate. For this son of mine was dead and is alive again" (Lk 15:22-24).

The son in that story is anyone who has rebelled against the love of God. That means all of us. The father is God, an all-forgiving God, not a celestial tyrant whose sole task is to give us a good thrashing whenever it appears we may be starting to enjoy ourselves.

Jesus knows the hurt, pain, depression and despair that come when we wander away from his love. Like the father in Christ's story, the arms of God are open wide. It's not difficult telling people about this love, but it is difficult getting them to accept it. When all the props are still in place, it's hard to see your need.

Fourth, *sin is ignoring God and neglecting other people.* Sin is apathy toward the truth. Just before his crucifixion, Jesus told his disciples what would happen when he returned in power. He would bring all the nations together and then put those who followed him on one side and those who didn't on the other. Then he will say to his people, "Come, you who are blessed by my Father; take your inheritance, the kingdom prepared for you since the creation of the world. For I was hungry and you gave me something to eat, I was thirsty and you gave me something to drink, I was a stranger and you invited me in, I needed clothes and you clothed me, I was sick and you looked after me, I was in prison and you came to visit me." But the people are astonished. They say to Christ that they never fed him or clothed him or tended to him when he was sick.

Christ then responds, "I tell you the truth, whatever you

did for one of the least of these brothers of mine, you did for me."

The other group is then told that they never helped Jesus when he was in need and are therefore cast out of the kingdom. And this group is equally shocked since they say they never saw Christ hungry or thirsty or sick or in prison either. His second answer is similar to his first. " 'I tell you the truth, whatever you did not do for one of the least of these, you did not do for me.' Then they will go away to eternal punishment, but the righteous to eternal life" (Mt 25:31-46).

Jesus attacked our indifference at all levels. Once we become his followers he does not allow us to be spectators or to stand on the sidelines and not get involved.

Christ has commanded us to love others, and love means action. It means we have to get our hands dirty, to immerse ourselves in the lives of hurting people. Followers of Jesus Christ are called to do more than give a good reason for their faith. We're called to serve and to help others, to meet the physical, emotional and spiritual wastelands so many people find themselves in.

I have seen people all over the country hear the message of Christ and do more than simply assent to his existence. Many of them are willing to allow his love to melt the neglect and apathy that once ruled their lives, and they allow him to thrust them into the world as Christ's agents of love, justice and righteousness.

Question 34. Why do Christians think they know how other people should live?

At Harvard University a student angrily asked me, "Why do you Christians think you have the absolute and final answer to everything? You talk as if there is no struggle in life, as if everything has been neatly packaged and cleanly cut."

Sometimes people will hear very regimented answers from Christians about how people should live. They may have heard rules about dancing and listening to contemporary music, playing cards and the like. Now while there may be good reasons for avoiding such things, we must be careful not to claim more than the Bible does. We certainly believe that God has given us absolute truth in the Bible. But we should never say that we know all truth. There are a lot of fuzzy areas in the world, even for Christians who believe there is a lot of clearcut right and wrong. It is important to answer this kind of inquiry carefully and deliberately. If this isn't done, the individual's perspective on Christian credibility will only be diminished further.

I told this student that a follower of Christ should understand that Jesus laid down very few absolute rules. The place to go to see a lot of detailed laws and regulations is city hall. Even in a country that prides itself on freedom, we have thousands upon thousands of laws regulating all kinds of activities.

Christians are people who have realized that by themselves they are incapable of living the kind of life God demands. Because they have come to this realization, they have accepted Christ's offer of forgiveness and a chance to start over. Even though they know that perfection is beyond their capability, they seek to live a life in obedience to Jesus Christ, knowing they will receive his guidance.

Because they are servants of Christ, Christians struggle constantly with some of the gray areas of life. For example, I struggle with the issue of money. How much should I keep? How much should I give to the poor? What should I buy for my family materially? What is extravagance? What is not?

When we accept Jesus Christ and become a Christian our power to reason and think does not go away. Christ does not take away our opportunity and our freedom to make choices on how to live our lives. We will not only continually struggle with the gray areas of life but also with the absolutes Christ has laid down. Becoming a Christian is not a passport to a mindless, choice-free way of existence. It is a call to follow a God who offers us the strength to make the right choices, and grace and forgiveness in abundance when we fall short.

Suggested Reading

Charles Durham. *Temptation.* Downers Grove, Ill.: InterVarsity Press, 1982.

Peter Kreeft. *The Best Things in Life.* Downers Grove, Ill.: InterVarsity Press, 1984.

John White. *Eros Defiled.* Downers Grove, Ill.: InterVarsity Press, 1977.

Earl Wilson. *Sexual Sanity.* Downers Grove, Ill.: InterVarsity Press, 1984.

Eight

Why Should I Believe in Christ?

When questions *about the Bible and hell and evil and* lifestyle have all been answered, it is common to hear some very broad concerns from people. These may sound like questions we have already discussed. But if someone has listened this far, they are likely asking how they fit in with God and what the implications for them would be of turning their lives over to Christ. So the following questions will deal more with the personal implications of believing in Christ.

Question 35. Why would God love someone like me?

Imagine for a moment that you live back in the time of Jesus. Imagine further that you have leprosy, a disease that is rare today but which back then meant a very slow and wasting death—the flesh goes numb and the extremities of the body begin to rot and fall off. Add to this horror the fact that you are an outcast. Every time you walk down the street you must shout out, "Unclean, unclean," so people can get out of your way and not be contaminated by your disease.

Into this setting comes Jesus Christ. You've heard stories of this man. His reputation has preceded him. You've heard of his power to heal. And so you move through the throngs of people, yelling, "Unclean," at the top of your lungs. You know Jesus is in the middle of the crowd, and you're desperate. You want to get to him. You may not have much power as a leper, but at least you can clear a room or break up a crowd faster than most people.

Finally you reach the feet of Jesus. You're broken, deserted and hopeless. You think that with Jesus you just might have a chance, but you also know that if he turns you down and walks away, you're finished. It's over. Through your tears you cry out, "Jesus, if you want to, you can make me clean."

Then something you've never seen before begins to happen. You see a hand reaching out to clasp your shoulder. Instinctively you draw back, not wanting to infect this man. But the hand grasps you anyway, and stays there for what seems an eternity.

From above you a voice says simply, "I want to. Be clean."

This is a story of power, a story of love unleashed. I tell it often to those who simply cannot believe they are worth God's attention, his love and the death of his Son. They believe God can love. He just can't love them. They feel that what they've done, or like the leper, who they are, makes them unlovable.

The wonderful promise of Scripture is that God is bigger than anything we can do that's wrong. God can reach deeper than any pit we can dig for ourselves. We cannot commit a sin that God cannot forgive.

Two apostles, Judas and Peter, are good examples of just how far God's care and forgiveness can reach. Peter was an individualist in every sense of the word. When the crowds were heading north, Peter was heading south. When every other apostle expressed apprehension about their devotion to Jesus, Peter jumped up and said, "Not me, Lord. I'd die for you in a minute. If everyone walks out the door on you, I'll stick around. Count on it."

Within minutes of Jesus' arrest in the garden of Gethsemane, Peter stood outside the home of the high priest and denied to three different people that he had ever known Christ. Pretty fickle, wasn't he? When Jesus was around, he was all full of love and devotion. When it came to putting his own skin on the line, he said, "Some other time."

As Jesus was being led to his death, he passed by where Peter was standing and their eyes met. Peter, knowing what he had just done, was crushed by the weight of his own guilt. He went out, wept bitterly and pleaded with God to forgive him. That is just what God did too. After the resurrection, Christ affirmed Peter's role in the church as a shepherd of his people (Jn 21:15-19).

Then there's the other apostle, Judas Iscariot, Christ's betrayer. Judas didn't deny Christ verbally and publicly. Instead he acted as a bounty hunter and sold Christ to the authorities for thirty pieces of silver.

Judas was also crushed with his own guilt when he recognized what he had done. But, unlike Peter, he didn't ask for forgiveness. Instead ne took the job upon himself of punishing and judging his act, and so committed suicide. How ironic that the one Judas betrayed paid the same price, death—the death designed to bring Judas to repentance and life!

Many of the people I speak with consider themselves to be like Judas and Peter. They are going through enormous guilt and don't know where to turn for comfort. Like the two apostles, they have a choice. Both Peter and Judas betrayed Jesus and denied him. Both of them deserved eternal punishment. Yet one man chose to be his own judge, jury and executioner. The other chose to turn and face his sin in all its ugliness and ask for forgiveness. He is remembered as the impetuous, beloved disciple who spoke boldly for Christ, and became a pillar of the church.

God loves each of us as much as he loved Peter. There is no sin too big that he can't forgive. He wants to forgive us. He's able to forgive us. He's ready to forgive us.

Question 36. Isn't the world hopeless?

Many people want to know what to do when their friends,

money and good looks finally fail them. They want to know if the God I speak about can offer any hope. They want to know if the God I speak about can do anything about the guilt that has drained all the joy and spontaneity out of their lives. They are asking for some hope.

Hope is the missing ingredient in many people's lives. A Russian student at Northwestern University in Chicago confronted me and said, "I am an atheist. I do not believe in your God, and I reject your Jesus. Life is simply an accident, and the morality you speak of is all relative. There is no hope."

But he went on to say, "I am afraid that Americans do not have the courage to face up to the logical conclusions of their atheism. I hear too much about meaning in life as if it really existed. I hear too much about moral absolutes. I hear too much about life after death. Few atheists in your country have the courage to face up to the despair of their atheism."

I respect this student's intellectual consistency. He had the courage to face the consequences of his beliefs. Many don't. They flee down the alley of agnosticism. They worship the search for God, telling us that it is impossible to know whether or not God exists. All they are doing is postponing the day when they will have to face the hopelessness their belief eventually will require of them.

I came across an even starker example of hopelessness at Brown University in Providence, Rhode Island. There a group of student leaders proposed that suicide pills be stocked in the health clinic to be given out in the event of a nuclear holocaust. They felt that if they survived such an incident, the aftereffects would be too painful to face.

No wonder we want to know if God has said anything that

would change our lives. The great truth of history is that God has spoken—first in the Old Testament through the writers of the law and the prophets. And he has spoken most clearly when he became one of us. John opens his gospel with the words, "In the beginning was the Word, and the Word was with God, and the Word was God." The author of the letter to the Hebrews begins, "In the past God spoke to our forefathers through the prophets at many times and in various ways, but in these last days he has spoken to us by his Son."

We can hope because God who is above history has spoken in history. He is over the nations. He is over presidents and prime ministers and kings. He is bringing all of history together under the rule of Jesus Christ. He will judge the righteous and the wicked. For those who follow him, there is indeed great hope.

Question 37. Who is the real Jesus?

Jesus the revolutionary! Gentle Jesus meek and mild. Jesus the great preacher. Jesus the faith healer. Jesus of the political right. Jesus of the political left.

It makes you weary just thinking about all these caricatures of Christ, doesn't it? How can anyone possibly come to a conclusion about this Jesus with all these diverse pictures floating around? It gets difficult at times to cut through all the slush and get to the heart of these questions. People hear Christians using the words of Christ in support of nuclear armament and in support of disarmament. They hear members of the clergy quote him to advocate apartheid and to speak against it. They hear Christians who speak vehemently in favor of pro-life and those who speak vehemently in favor of pro-choice. We tell them to believe in Jesus. But they want to know which Jesus they are supposed to follow

I find it best to start by describing some of his character qualities. One of the first is his compassion and willingness to forgive. To illustrate, consider the story of Jesus at a banquet attended by the religious elite of the community (Lk 7:40-50). I imagine that the conversation was subdued and that everyone was relaxed.

Into this setting burst one of the town prostitutes. She immediately went to where Jesus was sitting and began to weep. She fell to the floor by him and continued to cry unashamedly, letting her tears fall on his feet and wiping them dry with her hair.

The religious people stared in astonishment and indignation at this display. A few of them even thought, "If this man were a prophet, as he says he is, he would know who was touching him and exactly what kind of a woman she is— a filthy sinner."

Jesus knew what they were thinking and then directed his attention toward Simon, the host of the banquet. "Simon," he said, "I have a little story I want to tell you. There was a rich man who had two debtors. One owed him 500 days wages, another 50 days wages. Neither of them had any money to pay him back. Instead of demanding what was due him, he cancelled both of the debts.

"Now you tell me, Simon. Which of these two poor men loved the rich man more?"

"It's obvious," Simon replied. "The man who had the larger debt cancelled."

"Exactly," Jesus said. "Simon, I came to your house and you had no water to wash my feet, as is the custom. But this woman has not stopped washing my feet with her tears. I came to your house and you had no kiss of greeting, as is the custom. But this woman has not stopped kissing my feet. I came to your house and you had no oil to anoint my head, as is our custom. But this woman has not stopped anointing my feet with perfume.

"Therefore I tell you, her many sins have been forgiven, for she loved much. But he who has been forgiven little, loves little."

Then Jesus looked at the woman and said, "Your sins are forgiven."

The other guests began to say among themselves, "Who is this who even forgives sins?"

But Jesus went on to say to her, "Your faith has saved you. Go in peace."

Many people I speak to think Jesus is the God of those who have it together—the God of the well-groomed, of the scholar, of the athlete, of the well-behaved, of the well-organized. Sadly, there are enough Christians perpetrating this false picture to give it credibility.

But nothing could be further from the truth. The only thing Jesus asks of us is to accept what he has done for us in his death and resurrection. He asks us to accept the grace and forgiveness he freely offers. We come to Christ as we are. No haircut, no trimmed beard, no big income, no new wardrobe will make us any more acceptable than we are right now. His compassion is freely available.

Another quality of Jesus is his integrity. He didn't bother with a lot of the political and power games we play even though he had every opportunity to do so. He could easily have succumbed to Satan's temptations to be a high-and-mighty ruler of the entire earth. He could have donned the robes of the Pharisees and spent his days in idle philosophical conversation in the Temple. He could have walked among the people and been given all the dignity and respect anyone could possibly want.

Jesus could have been a king; he could have been wealthy. There are several occasions in Scripture in which the masses of people sought to make him king by force, by acclamation. Each time, however, he managed to slip away. All the treasures of the world could have been his, yet the Scriptures say, "The Son of man had no place to lay his head."

Jesus could have had it all. Instead he chose to concentrate on the mission his Father in heaven had given him— to heal the sick, not the healthy; to save the lost, not those who think they are okay. He would not compromise himself or his task to gain the world's recognition.

Christ also possessed the qualities of a servant. Through his example, Jesus asks us to die to that part of ourselves that would assert our false notions of supremacy and superiority. If you're like me, that's a big part of your personality. But Jesus is saying, "It's the least among you who will be the greatest. It's the one who assumes the posture of a servant that is the greatest."

The world teaches us exactly the opposite. The world tells me that I should assert myself. As I assert Cliffe's personality, then I will be a leader. Christ's answer to this is a simple no. He says, "As you learn to serve others, whether it is at the bottom or at the top of an organization, then I can use you."

Jesus also had the attitude of humility. Humility means forgetting to concentrate solely on my goals and priorities. It means becoming God-oriented in my goals rather than self-oriented—to say, "What will this action of mine do to further God's kingdom rather than, "How can I advance myself by this move?"

That's difficult to do because the world teaches us that unless we look out for number one, unless we intimidate and get ahead, no one will do it for us.

Again, Christ says no. In Matthew 6:33 he says, "But seek first his kingdom and his righteousness, and all these things will be given to you as well." "All these things" refer to food, shelter and clothing and yes, our self-esteem. This is one of the greatest promises in all Scripture and also one of the problems that requires the greatest amount of faith. If we act on this verse, humble ourselves, and accept the promise of God's provision, I believe our amazement will encourage our faith.

There are many other important characteristics of Jesus that we could consider. But the last one I would like to mention is his respect for the dignity of human life. We are worth dignity and respect not because of what we have accomplished, not because of how far we have advanced our careers, but because we are created in the image of God. We are also worth dignity and respect because God has put a price on our heads, the death of his only son, Jesus Christ.

Human dignity is the importance God attaches to us, and the importance he asks us to attach to each other. God judges us worthy because we are created in his image and he has paid a dear price for our redemption.

Most of us, on the other hand, tend to judge each other by outward appearances—clothing, income, physical stature, clarity of speech. It is shattering to think of all the human beauty and triumph we miss by concentrating most on the items God concentrates on least.

Jesus touched lepers, befriended outcasts and boldly criticized those corrupted by power. He expects us to do as he would—to hang our reputations on the line, to go where he would go, to do what he would do. There will not necessarily be any applause. But there will certainly be the peace of obedience granted to us.

If we want to know who Jesus is, we can't expect to find him wearing our favorite views, our political beliefs and our pet prejudices. He will arrive with the characteristics of compassion, integrity, humility and a respect for life. Remember, it is our task to conform to his agenda, not he to ours.

Question 38. Can't I wait and accept Christ later?

People often want to postpone commitment, especially a spiritual commitment. First, too many people have the false notion that when they accept Christ they will have to wear a sign around their neck that says, "I would rather be a Christian than be happy." Christ says that real joy comes from a relationship with God and relationships with people. Christ offers the deepest joy possible today.

Second, the Bible promises tomorrow to no one. Tonight one of the little blood vessels in my brain could rupture and I would pass into eternity. It is arrogant to assume that I am powerful enough to keep my life going for another year. That is totally beyond my control. The Bible teaches, "It is appointed unto man once to die. After that there is the judgment" (Heb 9:27). Our lives are the time God has given us to decide where we will spend eternity. After death there

ARLENE
MARKS HER
CALENDAR TO
CONSIDER
SPIRITUAL
MATTERS
A WEEK
FROM TUESDAY.

is no second chance, only the judgment.

Third, the only reason people seriously consider Christ is because the Holy Spirit is drawing them to Christ. If we turn a deaf ear to the quiet voice within us calling us to Christ today, we may become so hardened that we could never hear his voice later in life. Christ has not played games with us. He set his face toward Jerusalem, dealt with severe anguish in the garden of Gethsemane, went through a mockery of a trial, and bled and died on a cross to offer us forgiveness. We cannot make the mistake of treating him lightly. We cannot play games with Christ.

Fourth, Christ claimed, "I am the truth." To live apart from him is to live a lie. Satan deceives and distorts life. Christ calls us to live a life of truth. It is only as we commit our lives to Christ that we can become truly free and whole people. Jesus said, "The thief comes only to steal and kill and destroy. I have come that they may have life, and have it to the full" (Jn 10:10). Fulfillment in life today is found in commitment to Christ today.

Question 39. Why do I have to change when I become a Christian?

No one likes to change. And sometimes people will be reluctant to follow Christ because they recognize the demands he will be placing on their lifestyles. That is what is behind the questions about behavior that we covered in the last chapter.

And it is true. Christ does ask us to give up our old ways

when we come to him. He asks us to start seeing the world with different eyes.

Jesus taught the truth and lived out the truth perfectly. His teachings run at constant odds with the trends of our culture. Our culture says, "Be strong. Be utterly independent." Jesus said, "Blessed are the poor in spirit, for theirs is the kingdom of heaven. . . . Blessed are the meek, for they shall inherit the earth. . . . Who ever wants to become great among you must be your servant" (Mt 5:3, 5; 20:26).

We must come to Jesus with genuine humility. He poignantly demonstrated this quality himself to his disciples at the Last Supper. He took the towel and the basin and washed the dirt from their feet. The towel and the basin were commands from Jesus. He was showing us how we are to love one another. His act is a reminder that the selfishness in us must be consumed if we are ever to grow in holiness toward God and service toward others (Jn 13:1-17).

How am I to live right now? Jesus answered this very plainly when he said, "A new commandment I give you: Love one another. As I have loved you, so you must love one another" (Jn 13:34). A tall order? It sure is. It's easy for me to love those people who treat me kindly, who have similar interests, and who are continually affirming me. I have no trouble doing that at all. But that's not enough. Christ tells me that I must love others, even as he loved me. That includes those people who are hard to love; that includes people who do not treat us with care and concern; that includes those people we consider "beneath us." To imitate Christ means to love all people with a love that never fails.

Question 40. I'm happy. Why do I need Jesus?

I have three questions to ask people who think they don't need Christ since they are already happy. First, *What is the basis of your value and dignity as a human being?* A lot of people think, "I'll prove my value. I'll get money. I'll have sex. I will be macho. I will be sexy. I'll be a success." This, however, is a dangerous philosophy. If our value and dignity depends on our personal success, we are setting ourselves up for failure. How do we know that we will always be on the top? Does this mean that when we begin to fail that our value as human beings depreciates? Victor Frankl who survived the Auschwitz concentration camp said that the nihilism of the nineteenth century led to the death camps of the twentieth century. Even now there is a nihilistic tendency to devalue and depreciate that which is human.

Jesus teaches that we are valuable, that we have dignity because we are created in the image of God. In fact we are so valuable to God that even when we turned our backs on him, he did not turn his back on us. Instead he humbled himself and became man, lived a perfect life and then died on a cross for us. That is how valuable we are!

Racquel Welch, the media sex goddess said, "I am just a piece of meat. I fulfill the ambitions of other people to make money out of me." Fun, isn't it? What a wonderful life to view yourself as a piece of meat, as an object that fulfills the ambitions of other people. Jesus Christ challenges people to face up to the hollowness, the superficiality of life without God. And Jesus has his arms wide open calling broken, fractured, devalued, depreciated people to himself to find their true value, their true dignity.

The second question is, *What does real happiness come from?* Faye Dunaway, the beautiful movie actress, was in Lincoln Center in New York City attending a great gathering of famous people. A newspaper reporter asked Faye, "Are you happy?"

She responded, "I grew up in a small Midwest town. I was taught the American dream. Aim at success and once you attain it, then you'll be happy. Here I am among all the famous actors and actresses in New York City, but where is happiness?"

On another occasion Racquel Welch said, "I thought it was very peculiar that I had acquired everything I had wanted as a child—wealth, fame and accomplishment in my career. I had beautiful children and a lifestyle that seemed terrific, and yet I was totally and miserably unhappy. I found it very frightening that one could acquire all these things and still be so miserable."

You and I receive happiness from our relationships with other people. A relationship with a boyfriend, girlfriend, neighbor, roommate or family member brings great joy to life. Jesus Christ taught that ultimate joy comes from a deep love relationship with the living God. Don't believe the lie that teaches us that we find happiness by getting more money, having more sexual encounters, going to more parties and getting a little more drunk. Yes, there is a thrill to all of these, but the thrill fades. There is a superficiality to that type of thrill that is frightening.

My third question is simple: *If you are so happy, if you enjoy life so much, then how do you deal with death?* Tennessee Williams, the great playwright, once said,

"Whether or not we admit it to ourselves, we are all haunted by a truly awful sense of impermanence. I have always had a particularly keen sense of this at New York cocktail parties, and perhaps that is why I drink martinis almost as fast as I can snatch them from the tray. Fear and evasion are the two little beasts that chase each other's tails in the revolving wire cage of our nervous world."

Jesus' perspective is very different. He said, "Do not let your hearts be troubled. Trust in God; trust also in me. In my Father's house are many rooms; if it were not so, I would have told you. I am going there to prepare a place for you. And if I go and prepare a place for you, I will come back and take you to be with me that you also may be where I am. You know the way to the place where I am going."

One of his disciples said to him, "Lord, we don't know where you are going, so how can we know the way?"

Jesus replied, "I am the way and the truth and the life. No one comes to the Father except through me" (Jn 14:1-6).

You and I have lost our way. You and I have gotten mixed up. But God is so concerned about us in our mixed-up state that he has sent a clear message to us. He wrapped that message up in a person, his only son, Jesus Christ. Jesus revealed that there is a way through death out the other side to eternal life. Jesus revealed that there is a way to deal honestly and forthrightly with fear and anxiety. He showed us that the way to heaven, the way to life eternal, the way to overcome fear and anxiety, was to trust in him. Jesus never made a promise that he broke. He lived a life of total honesty. Today that same Jesus Christ offers you a quality of life that no one or thing can match.

Question 41. How is Jesus relevant to me?

Jesus lived two thousand years ago. That is literally ancient history to millions of people. How does he make a difference to us today? As human beings, we must deal with three basic questions: Where do I come from? How am I to live? Where am I going? Jesus answers those three basic human questions as no one else can.

First, where do I come from? I have been created in the image of God. But he did not make me and the world and send us spinning into orbit alone. No. He came with us and continues to interact with us.

But we rebelled against him. We rejected him and said we could live life just fine without him, thank you. The good news is that God is still trying to bring us back to him. We are so valuable to him that he was willing to die to win us back. God refuses to leave us alone.

Ethel Waters knew what loneliness was. She was born after her mother, a girl of fourteen, was raped. "A child growing up needs laps to cuddle up in," she said. "That never happened to me, never. It's a real tragic hurt wanting to be wanted so bad." But after she committed her life fully to Jesus Christ she said, "I keep praising the Lord so much I don't have any other hobbies." Jesus filled her with a deep sense of the presence of God that flowed out of her life in various expressions of deep joy.

I remember vividly when I was nine years old I was separated from my family when I spent a couple of weeks with my aunt and uncle. One day my cousin had an argument with my aunt. My aunt went upstairs and my cousin went running out the front door. I was left alone, a nine-year-old boy. I'll never forget walking down some stairs, overcome with loneliness. I began to weep. For the first time in my life I cried out from the depth of my being, "Jesus Christ, if you're really there I want to know it. I'm lonely and I hate it. If you're just a tradition that my parents have cleverly brainwashed me into believing, then we're going to bag this whole God bit now. But if you're really there, I want to know it." Instantly, a deep sense of the presence of Christ came over me. My nine-year-old tears dried up. I continued walking down the stairs but now I knew that I no longer walked alone. I had established contact with the living God.

To those who put their faith in him Jesus says, "Surely I am with you always, to the very end of the age" (Mt 28:20). Do you know where you come from? Do you know your roots? Do you know the Creator who created you, who loves you, who's bought you back, who offers you forgiveness and eternal life? Do you know Jesus Christ?

The second question is, How am I to live today. Jesus said, "A new commandment I give you: Love one another. As I have loved you, so you must love one another" (Jn 14:33). The apostle Paul clearly defined the love of Christ when he wrote in 1 Corinthians 13, "Love is patient, love is kind. It does not envy, it does not boast, it is not proud. It is not rude, it is not self-seeking, it is not easily angered, it keeps no record of wrongs. Love does not delight in evil but rejoices with the truth. It always protects, always trusts, always hopes, always perseveres. Love never fails" (vv. 4-8). That is the quality of love that our lives are to exhibit today.

Bertrand Russell once said, "Love your enemies is good advice, but too difficult for us." But Jesus said, "If anyone loves me, he will obey my teaching. My father will love him, and we will come to him and make our home with him" (Jn 14:23). When you receive Christ into your life God takes up residence within you and begins to give you the moral power to love as God created you to. When the love of Christ controls a human being, that person is intensely concerned about righteousness, justice, goodness, kindness. A follower of Jesus Christ is someone who is possessed by a desire to know and to live out truth.

The third question is, Where am I going? What does the future hold? Is there life after death or is death the end? We know that death is the great equalizer, but is there life after death?

In an interview in *Time* magazine, Woody Allen said, "In real life everyone gives himself a distraction, whether it's by turning on the TV set or by playing sophisticated games. You have to deny the reality of death to go on every day." George Bernard Shaw wrote, "Death is the ultimate statistic. One out of one die."

The American novelist Raymond Chandler wrote a book called *The Big Sleep,* "What did it matter where you lay when you were dead? In a dirty sump or in a marble tower on top of a high hill? You were dead, you were sleeping the big sleep, you were not bothered by things like that. Oil and water were the same as wind and air to you. You just slept the big sleep, not caring about the nastiness of how you died or where you fell."

On several occasions I've had people say, "I'm not afraid to die. When you die, that's it. It's not really a big deal." I especially remember one student, a very athletic-looking guy, giving me the same I-am-not-afraid line. Later in my week at that campus, some other students told me how much different his reaction was when he found he might have to face the draft. All of a sudden he began talking about reincarnation and life after death. The thought of a foreign bullet aimed straight at his brain didn't sit so well.

The Christian's belief in life after death is based on the historical evidence of the resurrection of Jesus Christ from the dead. It is not his plan for us to live seventy or eighty years and then pass off into oblivion. It is not his desire that we pass off into a cold and dark cosmos. He has created us to be immortal beings and given us the choice as to whether or not we will follow him or go our own way.

Jesus is relevant to each one of us. He does answer the most significant questions humans can ask. And he answers them fully in a way that will satisfy our hearts and our minds.

Suggested Reading

Michael Green. *The Empty Cross of Jesus.* Downers Grove, Ill.: InterVarsity Press, 1984.

John R. W. Stott. *Basic Christianity.* 2nd ed. Downers Grove, Ill.: InterVarsity Press, 1971.

Earl Wilson. *Does God Really Love Me?* Downers Grove, Ill.: InterVarsity Press, 1986.

Nine

How Can I Tell Others about Jesus?

Speaking with people *about Christ since my days in* junior high school has given me ample opportunity to learn from my mistakes. The example of wise believers has been an exciting educational experience As I have tried to introduce people to my closest friend, the Lord Jesus Christ, I have learned some ways to communicate more clearly my genuine love for them.

First, listening is of utmost importance in transmitting the gospel message. For the most part, people in our culture are self-centered and do not know how to listen. Sadly, many Christians who preach the gospel fall into that same category. A key part of loving those we talk to involves being genuinely interested in what they have to say. For the evangelist who seeks to build bridges and show the love of Christ, listening is paramount.

Second, discernment is needed to balance grace with truth. And that's always a difficult task. We must treat people with love and sensitivity, but we must also understand that the truth can hurt. We cannot go on an emotional roller coaster every time someone gets upset with us for presenting the truth. And it is inevitable that some will not like at all what we have to say to them. As Christ said, "Men loved darkness instead of light" (Jn 3:19). But we must work hard to be sure people are only upset with our message and not with the way we present our message.

A listening ear and discernment; those are two ingredients that must be in the portfolio of everyone who teaches and preaches the gospel. Combining love and truth, blending an attitude of listening with mental toughness—this is our task. Doing this will enable us to go on without getting burned out in our ministry.

A third principle in evangelism is to show how Christ touches all of life. One issue I continually speak about in my travels is justice. Those who talk with me are grateful that I raise issues such as apartheid and poverty. It often takes them by surprise. It helps them see that the gospel applies to all areas of life, that sin is not simply a matter of messing up in personal morality but also messing up in the public sphere. To hold the balance is not easy, but as a follower of Jesus Christ I am committed to seeing justice and righteousness achieved in the private and the public spheres.

Fourth, when I am answering students questions I try to break down some of the barriers they may have. Usually, when I finish my reply, be it an inquiry into the nature of God, or the way to God, I say, "Thank you for that good question." At first glance this may appear to be mere formality, like saying thanks after someone passes the butter.

But it's not. I see any inquiry, any question that seeks knowledge into God's nature, as being good. Granted, there are some belligerent and thoughtless questions thrown my way. But even so, someone is asking. There is at least a shred of interest. If they were completely apathetic they wouldn't have even asked a belligerent question. So I take them seriously.

My advice to Christians is to listen to all questions you are asked with an open mind and an open heart. Give those you talk to respect, even if the question seems very elementary to you. Though it may seem simple to you, it may loom as a huge barrier for someone who is seeking answers.

Last, don't think you have to be an open-air preacher to be a witness for Christ. Even though I am the one standing in front of a crowd answering questions, most of the conversions come when Christians sprinkled in the crowd engage people in conversation one on one. I can't follow everyone into their homes or apartments. But those in the local Christian community can do just that, befriending non-Christians, caring for them and loving them into the kingdom. Sometimes that takes hours, sometimes days, sometimes years. I rejoice in everyone who witnesses faithfully. I praise God for his body of believers who take his good news into the world. During my years in seminary, I preached in bars in inner city Boston. One night a newspaper reporter joined me. After a few seemingly fruitless conversations with people on the streets, in diners and in bars, the reporter said to me, "Cliffe, according to all my definitions of success and failure, you are a total failure. There have been no 'conversions.' Most people have seemed disinterested. How do you deal with that?"

I answered, "A person's coming to Christ is like a chain with many links. There is a first link, middle links and a last link. There are many influences and conversations that precede a person's decision to convert to Christ. I know the joy of being the first link at times, a middle link usually and occasionally the last link. God has not called me to only be the last link. He has called me to be faithful and to love all people. I have never converted anyone. That is the work of the Holy Spirit. It has been my privilege to be around occasionally when a person has responded to the Holy Spirit's tug. They have stepped across the line from death to life."

The reporter responded, "That is beginning to make some sense."

Often as I drove from Boston back to the seminary late Saturday night, I would ask myself, "How many conversions were there tonight?"

The answer was, "None."

So I would ask myself, "What of any consequence was accomplished by you tonight?"

The answer was often "Not much." But consistently, God's Word was a tremendous source of strength and courage. "Stand firm. Let nothing move you. Always give yourselves fully to the work of the Lord, because you know that your labor in the Lord is not in vain" (1 Cor 15:58).

Suggested Reading

Paul Little. *How to Give Away Your Faith.* Downers Grove, Ill.: InterVarsity Press, 1966.

Rebecca Manley Pippert. *Out of the Saltshaker.* Downers Grove, Ill.: InterVarsity Press, 1979.

Don Posterski. *Why Am I Afraid to Tell You I'm a Christian?* Downers Grove, Ill.: InterVarsity Press, 1983.